# JavaScript
## Advanced Programming (Second Edition)

### Thomas F. Elston

Over the past five years, Tom Elston's career has led him through many different facets of the IT training world at Element K.

As an award-winning editor, he has successfully edited titles ranging from the simplest of introductory texts to multi-day certification courseware on network administration and programming—all while steering projects through the company's break-neck migration from a conventional publishing production system to the bleeding-edge XML content management system currently in use.

As a writer, Mr. Elston has produced titles related to JavaScript, ColdFusion, and HomeSite, and has collaborated on the development of the company's line of Java courseware. He is also the resident subject-matter expert on Element K's E-Business curriculum.

In terms of online training, Mr. Elston is the co-developer of the set of online tutorials currently used by Macromedia for ColdFusion 5.0, its tag-based database application server. He has also been involved as an instructor in synchronous online training events hosted through the Element K Web site.

### Brian S. Wilson

Brian Wilson has developed more than 30 courses on computer programming, network administration, and end-user topics. He is a Renaissance man who continually reinvents himself. Brian has been an assembly-line worker; an HVAC mechanic; a technical writer; a security guard; a computer programmer; a high school English teacher; a remodeling contractor; and (for the last 11 years) an instructional designer. And at 6'3" and 300 pounds, he just might be large enough to be all those people at the same time. Brian holds a B.S. in English from SUNY College at Brockport, and an M.S. in Instructional Technology from Rochester Institute of Technology.

# JavaScript: Advanced Programming (Second Edition)

Course Number: 077972
Course Edition: 1.0
For software version: 1.5

## ACKNOWLEDGEMENTS

### Project Team

**Curriculum Developers and Technical Writers :** Brian S. Wilson and Thomas F. Elston • **Technical Editor :** Cory Brown • **Graphic Designers:** Daniel Smith and Isolina Salgado • **EPS Technician:** Debra A. Denison

### Project Support

**Development Assistance :** Tim Poulsen • **Content Manager:** Chris Clark

### Administration

**Senior Director of Content and Content Development:** William O. Ingle • **Director of Certification:** Mike Grakowsky • **Director of Design and Web Development:** Joy Insinna • **Manager of Office Productivity and Applied Learning:** Cheryl Russo • **Manager of Databases, ERP, and Business Skills:** Mark Onisk • **Director of Business Development:** Kent Michels • **Instructional Design Manager:** Susan L. Reber • **Manager of Publishing Services:** Michael Hoyt

## NOTICES

**DISCLAIMER:** While Element K Content LLC takes care to ensure the accuracy and quality of these materials, we cannot guarantee their accuracy, and all materials are provided without any warranty whatsoever, including, but not limited to, the implied warranties of merchantability or fitness for a particular purpose.

**TRADEMARK NOTICES:** Element K Content LLC, ZDU, FirstEdition, Element K Journals and the corresponding logos are trademarks and service marks of Element K Content LLC. JavaScript is a registered trademark of Netscape Communications Corporation. All other product names and services used throughout this book are common law or registered trademarks and service marks of their respective companies. Use of another entity's product name or service in this book is for editorial purposes only. No such use, or the use of any trade name, is intended to convey endorsement or other affiliation with the book.

Copyright © 2001 Element K Content LLC. All rights reserved. This publication, or any part thereof, may not be reproduced or transmitted in any form or by any means, electronic or mechanical, including photocopying, recording, storage in an information retrieval system, or otherwise, without express written permission of Element K Content LLC, 500 Canal View Boulevard, Rochester, NY 14623, (800) 434-3466. Element K Content LLC's World Wide Web site is located at **www.elementkpress.com**.

Unauthorized reproduction or transmission of any part of this book or materials is a violation of federal law. If you believe that this book, related materials, or any other Element K Content LLC materials are being reproduced or transmitted without permission, please call 1-800-478-7788.

**HELP US IMPROVE OUR COURSEWARE**

Your comments are important to us. Please contact us at Element K Press LLC, 1-800-478-7788, 500 Canal View Boulevard, Rochester, NY 14623, Attention: Product Planning, or through our Web site at **http://support.elementkpress.com**.

# JavaScript: Advanced Programming (Second Edition)

# Content Overview

| | |
|---|---|
| About This Course | vii |
| Lesson 1: Error-handling and Debugging | 1 |
| Lesson 2: Custom Objects | 33 |
| Lesson 3: Arrays | 49 |
| Lesson 4: Displaying and Manipulating Data Tables | 69 |
| Lesson 5: Cookies | 93 |
| Lesson 6: Communicating With Applets | 115 |
| Appendix A: JavaScript and Server Applications | 129 |
| Solutions | 133 |
| Glossary | 143 |
| Index | 145 |

# CONTENTS

# JavaScript: Advanced Programming (Second Edition)

## Contents

About This Course .................................................... vii
Course Setup Information ............................................. viii
How To Use This Book ................................................. xv

## Lesson 1: Error-handling and Debugging

**Topic 1A  Common Scripting Errors** ................................. 2

**Topic 1B  Using the Microsoft Windows Script Debugger** ............ 8
    Check Your Skills 1-1 ......................................... 11
    Check Your Skills 1-2 ......................................... 14
    Check Your Skills 1-3 ......................................... 17

**Topic 1C  Language-based Debugging and Error Handling** ........... 24
    Apply Your Knowledge 1-1 ...................................... 30
    Lesson Review 1 ............................................... 30

## Lesson 2: Custom Objects

**Topic 2A  Introduction to Objects** ................................ 34

**Topic 2B  Constructor Functions** .................................. 37
    Check Your Skills 2-1 ......................................... 39

**Topic 2C  Methods** ............................................... 40
    Check Your Skills 2-2 ......................................... 42
    Apply Your Knowledge 2-1 ...................................... 42
    Lesson Review 2 ............................................... 47

# CONTENTS

## LESSON 3: ARRAYS

| Topic 3A | Introduction to Arrays | 50 |
| Topic 3B | Creating and Populating Arrays | 52 |
| Topic 3C | Deleting Array Elements | 57 |
| Topic 3D | Multi-dimensional Arrays | 59 |
| | Apply Your Knowledge 3-1 | 63 |
| | Lesson Review 3 | 67 |

## LESSON 4: DISPLAYING AND MANIPULATING DATA TABLES

| Topic 4A | Loading Data | 70 |
| Topic 4B | Selecting Data for Display | 77 |
| Topic 4C | Searching Data for Display | 81 |
| Topic 4D | Sorting Data for Display | 86 |
| | Lesson Review 4 | 91 |

## LESSON 5: COOKIES

| Topic 5A | Introduction to the Cookie Object | 94 |
| Topic 5B | Storing Cookies | 98 |
| Topic 5C | Reading and Processing Cookie Values | 102 |
| Topic 5D | Deleting Cookies | 107 |
| | Apply Your Knowledge 5-1 | 109 |
| | Lesson Review 5 | 112 |

## LESSON 6: COMMUNICATING WITH APPLETS

| Topic 6A | Communicating With Java Applets | 116 |
| Topic 6B | Communicating With Director Shockwave Movies | 119 |
| Topic 6C | Communicating with ActiveX | 124 |
| | Lesson Review 6 | 126 |

Contents  v

# CONTENTS

## Appendix A: JavaScript and Server Applications

**Communicating With Server Applications** .........................129

**Solutions** .....................................................133

**Glossary** .....................................................143

**Index** .......................................................145

# INTRODUCTION

## ABOUT THIS COURSE

Welcome to the Element K Content training team.

Our goal is to provide you with the best computer training available and we know exactly what that takes. Our corporate heritage is based in training. In fact, we use our Student Manuals every day, in classes just like yours, so you can be confident that the material has been tested and proven to be effective.

If you have any suggestions on how we can improve our products or services, please contact us.

# ABOUT THIS COURSE

*JavaScript: Advanced Programming (Second Edition)* is a hands-on instruction book for students who want to learn more about JavaScript programming.

## Course Prerequisites

Before they begin this course, students should understand basic JavaScript programming. For example, they should already know how to write and call a simple JavaScript function.

We do not provide basic computer, Internet, or JavaScript concepts in this book. A student who hasn't used JavaScript should first take the Element K course *JavaScript: Programming (Second Edition)*.

## Course Objectives

When you're done working your way through this book, you'll be able to:

- Debug code and handle errors.
- Create custom objects with custom methods and properties.
- Create, read to, write from, and delete both single and multi-dimensional arrays.
- Build functionality that selects, sorts, and searches data tables for display.
- Store, retrieve, and delete cookies.
- Write JavaScript code to communicate with Java applets, Shockwave movies, and ActiveX controls.

# ABOUT THIS COURSE

*This course was developed and tested in a Windows environment. Performance on other systems may vary.*

# COURSE SETUP INFORMATION

## Hardware and Software Requirements

To run this course, you will need:

- A PC-compatible (or Macintosh) computer.
- A Super VGA monitor and video card capable of displaying at a resolution of 800 x 600 or greater.
- A connection to the Internet.
- A mouse or compatible tracking device.
- A CD-ROM drive.
- For Internet Explorer 6:
— A computer with a 486/66 MHz processor or higher (Pentium recommended).
— RAM requirements (minimum):
    - On Windows 98: 16 MB.
    - On Windows 98 Second Edition: 16 MB.
    - On Windows NT 4.0 with Service Pack 6a and higher: 32 MB.
    - On Windows 2000: 32 MB.
    - On Windows Millennium Edition: 32 MB.
— Hard Drive Space (full install):
    - On Windows 98: 11.5 MB.
    - On Windows 98 Second Edition: 12.4 MB.
    - On Windows NT 4.0 with Service Pack 6a and higher: 12.7 MB.
    - On Windows 2000: 12 MB.
    - On Windows Millennium Edition: 8.7 MB.
- For Netscape Navigator 6.1:
— On Windows:
    - Windows 95, 98, 98SE, Millennium, NT 4.0, or 2000
    - Intel Pentium-class 233 MHz (or faster) processor
    - 64 MB RAM
    - 26 MB free hard disk space
— On Macintosh:
    - Mac OS 8.6 or later
    - PowerPC 604e 266 MHz or faster processor, or G3/G4
    - 64 MB RAM
    - 36 MB free hard disk space
— On Linux
    - Red Hat Linux 6.x and 7 with X11 R6
    - Intel Pentium-class 233 MHz (or faster) processor
    - 64 MB RAM

# ABOUT THIS COURSE

- 26 MB free hard disk space

**Note:** The next items are optional. If you want to review the material on CGI in Appendix A, you will have to set up a server.

- (For course setup only) Administrative access to a Web server (to install a server application and various demo files).
- Client access to a Web server (to submit CGI requests to a server application and to browse various demo files).

## Class Requirements

In order for the class to run properly, perform the procedures described below.

1. **Configure your computer's display** at 800 x 600 or greater resolution with at least 256 colors.

2. **Install Netscape Navigator 6.1 (or newer)** following the manufacturer's recommendations, performing all the configuration steps its setup program requires. (See **http://browsers.netscape.com/browsers/main.tmpl** to download the browser.)

   **Note:** Install Navigator before Internet Explorer. Otherwise, primary features of Internet Explorer, such as loading a page from a bookmark, might be usurped by Navigator.

3. **Install Internet Explorer 6.x (or newer)** following the manufacturer's recommendations, performing all the configuration steps its setup program requires. (See **http://www.microsoft.com/windows/ie/default.asp** to download the browser.)

4. **Install the data files for this course from the CD-ROM included with this book** by doing one of the following:
   - *For Windows* — Open the contents of the CD-ROM through My Computer and open the 077_972 folder. Open the Data folder contained within and double-click on the 077972dd.exe file to start the installation process. A folder labeled "JavaScript Adv Prog," which contains all the files for the course, will be created on your C:\ drive.
   - *For Macintosh* — Double-click on the CD-ROM icon and open the 077_972 folder. Open the Data folder contained within and drag the 077972dd.hqx file to your desktop. Double-click on the .hqx file to unstuff its contents. A folder labeled "077972dd" will be created on your desktop. Open this folder, and drag the "JavaScript Adv Prog" folder contained within to your hard disk. This folder contains all the files that you will use throughout the course.

5. If you plan to use HomeSite as the text editor for the course, **install it from the HomeSite folder**, located on the CD-ROM accompanying this text. **Configure the following settings in HomeSite:**
   - Turn on line numbers in the gutter;
   - Turn off tag insight, tag completion, and tag validation;
   - Set the default file extension to be `.html`;
   - Configure HomeSite to treat tabs as spaces;

*About This Course* **ix**

# ABOUT THIS COURSE

- Configure the code templates so that the JavaScript code block is listed first (change its keyword name to "a script");
- Configure the external browser list to recognize both Navigator and Internet Explorer as external browsers; and
- Set Navigator to be the primary external browser.

Detailed instructions for using HomeSite are included on the CD-ROM, as well. Simply run the HomeSite — How To.exe program, and open the homesite.html file in a browser in order to access these instructions.

Because HomeSite is a demonstration copy of the program, its license will expire after a period, forcing you to re-install the program. If you like the program and think it works well in class, please consider purchasing your own copy from Macromedia. You can purchase HomeSite from their Web site: **http://www.macromedia.com**. If you are unable to install HomeSite from the CD-ROM, check Macromedia's Web site for a trial version.

*For further information about the debugger, go to* **http://msdn.microsoft.com/scripting**

6. **Install the Microsoft Windows Script Debugger** as per the requirements listed on the Microsoft Web site. As of this writing, the download page for the debugger is: **http://msdn.microsoft.com/downloads/default.asp?url=/downloads/topic.asp?url=/msdn-files/028/001/175/topic.xml**.

7. If you plan to use a Web server:
   - Copy the entire contents of the JavaScript Adv Prog folder to a directory on the Web server. Note the URL for this directory; you will need it to access data files.
   - Copy CGIDEMO.EXE to a directory on the Web server (immediately off the root) named CGI-Bin. If you need to create this directory, configure the Web server so that server applications can be run from /CGI-Bin.

In addition to the specific setup procedures needed for this class to run properly, you should also check our Web site at **support.elementkpress.com** for more information. Any updates about this course will be posted there.

## List of Additional Files

On the first page of each lesson is a list of files that students open to complete the activities in the lesson. Following is a list of additional files that students don't open, but that are necessary for this course. Do not delete these files.

| Lesson | File name and path |
|---|---|
| 2 | Explore\Start.htm |
| 2 | Explore\Images\labpg.gif |
| 2 | Lab - Objects\Images\aAnvil.gif |
| 2 | Lab - Objects\Images\aBkpack.gif |
| 2 | Lab - Objects\Images\aBucket.gif |
| 2 | Lab - Objects\Images\aChemkit.gif |
| 2 | Lab - Objects\Images\aDrill.gif |
| 2 | Lab - Objects\Images\aGascan.gif |
| 2 | Lab - Objects\Images\aHammer.gif |

# ABOUT THIS COURSE

| | |
|---|---|
| 2 | Lab - Objects\Images\aLantern.gif |
| 2 | Lab - Objects\Images\aNa.gif |
| 2 | Lab - Objects\Images\Anvil.gif |
| 2 | Lab - Objects\Images\aOilCan.gif |
| 2 | Lab - Objects\Images\aPans.gif |
| 2 | Lab - Objects\Images\aPick.gif |
| 2 | Lab - Objects\Images\aSluice.gif |
| 2 | Lab - Objects\Images\banrbord.gif |
| 2 | Lab - Objects\Images\banrlogo.gif |
| 2 | Lab - Objects\Images\biglogo.gif |
| 2 | Lab - Objects\Images\Bkpack.gif |
| 2 | Lab - Objects\Images\bordlogo.gif |
| 2 | Lab - Objects\Images\bordlogo.jpg |
| 2 | Lab - Objects\Images\Bucket.gif |
| 2 | Lab - Objects\Images\Chemkit.gif |
| 2 | Lab - Objects\Images\Drill.gif |
| 2 | Lab - Objects\Images\Gascan.gif |
| 2 | Lab - Objects\Images\Hammer.gif |
| 2 | Lab - Objects\Images\Lantern.gif |
| 2 | Lab - Objects\Images\lillogo.gif |
| 2 | Lab - Objects\Images\mapbg.gif |
| 2 | Lab - Objects\Images\mapskchc.gif |
| 2 | Lab - Objects\Images\minebg.gif |
| 2 | Lab - Objects\Images\minebglt.gif |
| 2 | Lab - Objects\Images\Na.gif |
| 2 | Lab - Objects\Images\OilCan.gif |
| 2 | Lab - Objects\Images\Pans.gif |
| 2 | Lab - Objects\Images\Pick.gif |
| 2 | Lab - Objects\Images\sbanLogo.gif |
| 2 | Lab - Objects\Images\Sluice.gif |
| 2 | Lab - Objects\Images\tools.gif |
| 2 | Lab - Objects\Images\toolsbg.gif |
| 2 | Lab - Objects\Images\toolscut.gif |
| 2 | Lab - Objects\Images\xPans.gif |
| 3 | Explore\Start.htm |
| 3 | Explore\Images\labpg.gif |
| 3 | Explore\Arrays\Arrays.htm |
| 3 | Explore\Arrays\Arcode.htm |
| 3 | Lab - Arrays\Solution\matrix.js |
| 3 | Explore\Bugs\debug.js |
| 5 | Explore\Start.htm |
| 5 | Explore\Images\labpg.gif |
| 5 | Explore\LMSite\CatBanner.htm |
| 5 | Explore\LMSite\HomeLogo.htm |
| 5 | Explore\LMSite\CatContent.htm |
| 5 | Explore\LMSite\catalog.js |

*About This Course* **xi**

# ABOUT THIS COURSE

| | |
|---|---|
| 5 | Explore\LMSite\Cart.htm |
| 5 | Explore\LMSite\cookies.js |
| 5 | Explore\LMSite\dollars.js |
| 5 | Explore\LMSite\Images\aAnvil.gif |
| 5 | Explore\LMSite\Images\aBkpack.gif |
| 5 | Explore\LMSite\Images\aBucket.gif |
| 5 | Explore\LMSite\Images\aChemkit.gif |
| 5 | Explore\LMSite\Images\aDrill.gif |
| 5 | Explore\LMSite\Images\aGascan.gif |
| 5 | Explore\LMSite\Images\aHammer.gif |
| 5 | Explore\LMSite\Images\aLantern.gif |
| 5 | Explore\LMSite\Images\aNa.gif |
| 5 | Explore\LMSite\Images\Anvil.gif |
| 5 | Explore\LMSite\Images\aOilCan.gif |
| 5 | Explore\LMSite\Images\aPans.gif |
| 5 | Explore\LMSite\Images\aPick.gif |
| 5 | Explore\LMSite\Images\aSluice.gif |
| 5 | Explore\LMSite\Images\banrbord.gif |
| 5 | Explore\LMSite\Images\banrlogo.gif |
| 5 | Explore\LMSite\Images\biglogo.gif |
| 5 | Explore\LMSite\Images\Bkpack.gif |
| 5 | Explore\LMSite\Images\bordlogo.gif |
| 5 | Explore\LMSite\Images\bordlogo.jpg |
| 5 | Explore\LMSite\Images\Bucket.gif |
| 5 | Explore\LMSite\Images\Chemkit.gif |
| 5 | Explore\LMSite\Images\Drill.gif |
| 5 | Explore\LMSite\Images\Gascan.gif |
| 5 | Explore\LMSite\Images\Hammer.gif |
| 5 | Explore\LMSite\Images\Lantern.gif |
| 5 | Explore\LMSite\Images\lillogo.gif |
| 5 | Explore\LMSite\Images\mapbg.gif |
| 5 | Explore\LMSite\Images\mapskchc.gif |
| 5 | Explore\LMSite\Images\minebg.gif |
| 5 | Explore\LMSite\Images\minebglt.gif |
| 5 | Explore\LMSite\Images\Na.gif |
| 5 | Explore\LMSite\Images\OilCan.gif |
| 5 | Explore\LMSite\Images\Pans.gif |
| 5 | Explore\LMSite\Images\Pick.gif |
| 5 | Explore\LMSite\Images\sbanLogo.gif |
| 5 | Explore\LMSite\Images\Sluice.gif |
| 5 | Explore\LMSite\Images\tools.gif |
| 5 | Explore\LMSite\Images\toolsbg.gif |
| 5 | Explore\LMSite\Images\toolscut.gif |
| 5 | Explore\LMSite\Images\xPans.gif |
| 5 | Explore\Cookies\Cookiloc.htm |
| 5 | Lab - Cookies\Solution\CartFrame.htm |

# ABOUT THIS COURSE

| | | |
|---|---|---|
| 5 | Lab - Cookies\Solution\Catalog.js | |
| 5 | Lab - Cookies\Solution\CatBanner.htm | |
| 5 | Lab - Cookies\Solution\CatContent.htm | |
| 5 | Lab - Cookies\Solution\CatFrame.htm | |
| 5 | Lab - Cookies\Solution\CatLogo.htm | |
| 5 | Lab - Cookies\Solution\CatNav.htm | |
| 5 | Lab - Cookies\Solution\checkout.htm | |
| 5 | Lab - Cookies\Solution\cookies.js | |
| 5 | Lab - Cookies\Solution\dollars.js | |
| 5 | Lab - Cookies\Solution\HomeLogo.htm | |
| 5 | Lab - Cookies\Solution\howMuch.htm | |
| 5 | Lab - Cookies\Solution\shipcosts.js | |
| 5 | Lab - Cookies\Solution\stuffcat.js | |
| 5 | Lab - Cookies\CartFrame.htm | |
| 5 | Lab - Cookies\Catalog.js | |
| 5 | Lab - Cookies\CatBanner.htm | |
| 5 | Lab - Cookies\CatContent.htm | |
| 5 | Lab - Cookies\CatFrame.htm | |
| 5 | Lab - Cookies\CatLogo.htm | |
| 5 | Lab - Cookies\CatNav.htm | |
| 5 | Lab - Cookies\checkout.htm | |
| 5 | Lab - Cookies\cookies.js | |
| 5 | Lab - Cookies\dollars.js | |
| 5 | Lab - Cookies\howMuch.htm | |
| 5 | Lab - Cookies\shipcosts.js | |
| 5 | Lab - Cookies\stuffcat.js | |
| 5 | Lab - Cookies\Images\aAnvil.gif | |
| 5 | Lab - Cookies\Images\aBkpack.gif | |
| 5 | Lab - Cookies\Images\aBucket.gif | |
| 5 | Lab - Cookies\Images\aChemkit.gif | |
| 5 | Lab - Cookies\Images\aDrill.gif | |
| 5 | Lab - Cookies\Images\aGascan.gif | |
| 5 | Lab - Cookies\Images\aHammer.gif | |
| 5 | Lab - Cookies\Images\aLantern.gif | |
| 5 | Lab - Cookies\Images\aNa.gif | |
| 5 | Lab - Cookies\Images\Anvil.gif | |
| 5 | Lab - Cookies\Images\aOilCan.gif | |
| 5 | Lab - Cookies\Images\aPans.gif | |
| 5 | Lab - Cookies\Images\aPick.gif | |
| 5 | Lab - Cookies\Images\aSluice.gif | |
| 5 | Lab - Cookies\Images\banrbord.gif | |
| 5 | Lab - Cookies\Images\banrlogo.gif | |
| 5 | Lab - Cookies\Images\biglogo.gif | |
| 5 | Lab - Cookies\Images\Bkpack.gif | |
| 5 | Lab - Cookies\Images\bordlogo.gif | |
| 5 | Lab - Cookies\Images\bordlogo.jpg | |

# ABOUT THIS COURSE

| | |
|---|---|
| 5 | Lab - Cookies\Images\Bucket.gif |
| 5 | Lab - Cookies\Images\Chemkit.gif |
| 5 | Lab - Cookies\Images\Drill.gif |
| 5 | Lab - Cookies\Images\Gascan.gif |
| 5 | Lab - Cookies\Images\Hammer.gif |
| 5 | Lab - Cookies\Images\Lantern.gif |
| 5 | Lab - Cookies\Images\lillogo.gif |
| 5 | Lab - Cookies\Images\mapbg.gif |
| 5 | Lab - Cookies\Images\mapskchc.gif |
| 5 | Lab - Cookies\Images\minebg.gif |
| 5 | Lab - Cookies\Images\minebglt.gif |
| 5 | Lab - Cookies\Images\Na.gif |
| 5 | Lab - Cookies\Images\OilCan.gif |
| 5 | Lab - Cookies\Images\Pans.gif |
| 5 | Lab - Cookies\Images\Pick.gif |
| 5 | Lab - Cookies\Images\sbanLogo.gif |
| 5 | Lab - Cookies\Images\Sluice.gif |
| 5 | Lab - Cookies\Images\tools.gif |
| 5 | Lab - Cookies\Images\toolsbg.gif |
| 5 | Lab - Cookies\Images\toolscut.gif |
| 5 | Lab - Cookies\Images\xPans.gif |
| 5 | Lab - Cookies\Solution\Images\aAnvil.gif |
| 5 | Lab - Cookies\Solution\Images\aBkpack.gif |
| 5 | Lab - Cookies\Solution\Images\aBucket.gif |
| 5 | Lab - Cookies\Solution\Images\aChemkit.gif |
| 5 | Lab - Cookies\Solution\Images\aDrill.gif |
| 5 | Lab - Cookies\Solution\Images\aGascan.gif |
| 5 | Lab - Cookies\Solution\Images\aHammer.gif |
| 5 | Lab - Cookies\Solution\Images\aLantern.gif |
| 5 | Lab - Cookies\Solution\Images\aNa.gif |
| 5 | Lab - Cookies\Solution\Images\Anvil.gif |
| 5 | Lab - Cookies\Solution\Images\aOilCan.gif |
| 5 | Lab - Cookies\Solution\Images\aPans.gif |
| 5 | Lab - Cookies\Solution\Images\aPick.gif |
| 5 | Lab - Cookies\Solution\Images\aSluice.gif |
| 5 | Lab - Cookies\Solution\Images\banrbord.gif |
| 5 | Lab - Cookies\Solution\Images\banrlogo.gif |
| 5 | Lab - Cookies\Solution\Images\biglogo.gif |
| 5 | Lab - Cookies\Solution\Images\Bkpack.gif |
| 5 | Lab - Cookies\Solution\Images\bordlogo.gif |
| 5 | Lab - Cookies\Solution\Images\bordlogo.jpg |
| 5 | Lab - Cookies\Solution\Images\Bucket.gif |
| 5 | Lab - Cookies\Solution\Images\Chemkit.gif |
| 5 | Lab - Cookies\Solution\Images\Drill.gif |
| 5 | Lab - Cookies\Solution\Images\Gascan.gif |
| 5 | Lab - Cookies\Solution\Images\Hammer.gif |

# ABOUT THIS COURSE

| | |
|---|---|
| 5 | Lab - Cookies\Solution\Images\Lantern.gif |
| 5 | Lab - Cookies\Solution\Images\lillogo.gif |
| 5 | Lab - Cookies\Solution\Images\mapbg.gif |
| 5 | Lab - Cookies\Solution\Images\mapskchc.gif |
| 5 | Lab - Cookies\Solution\Images\minebg.gif |
| 5 | Lab - Cookies\Solution\Images\minebglt.gif |
| 5 | Lab - Cookies\Solution\Images\Na.gif |
| 5 | Lab - Cookies\Solution\Images\OilCan.gif |
| 5 | Lab - Cookies\Solution\Images\Pans.gif |
| 5 | Lab - Cookies\Solution\Images\Pick.gif |
| 5 | Lab - Cookies\Solution\Images\sbanLogo.gif |
| 5 | Lab - Cookies\Solution\Images\Sluice.gif |
| 5 | Lab - Cookies\Solution\Images\tools.gif |
| 5 | Lab - Cookies\Solution\Images\toolsbg.gif |
| 5 | Lab - Cookies\Solution\Images\toolscut.gif |
| 5 | Lab - Cookies\Solution\Images\xPans.gif |
| 6 | Explore\Start.htm |
| 6 | Explore\Images\labpg.gif |
| 6 | Explore\Applets\Java\slider.jar |
| 6 | Explore\Applets\SWave\control.dcr |
| 6 | Explore\Applets\ActiveX\xRemote.cab |
| 6 | Cgidemo.exe |

# HOW TO USE THIS BOOK

You can use this book as a learning guide, a review tool, and a reference.

## As a Learning Guide

Each lesson covers one broad topic or set of related topics. Lessons are arranged in order of increasing proficiency with JavaScript; skills you acquire in one lesson are used and developed in subsequent lessons. For this reason, you should work through the lessons in sequence.

We organized each lesson into explanatory topics and step-by-step activities. Topics provide the theory you need to master advanced JavaScript programming; activities allow you to apply this theory to practical hands-on examples.

You get to try out each new skill on a specially prepared sample file. This saves you typing time and allows you to concentrate on the technique at hand. Through the use of sample files, hands-on activities, illustrations that give you feedback at crucial steps, supporting background information, and independent labs and practices, this book provides you with the foundation and structure to learn JavaScript programming quickly and easily.

# ABOUT THIS COURSE

## As a Review Tool

Any method of instruction is only as effective as the time and effort you are willing to invest in it. For this reason, we encourage you to spend some time reviewing the book's more challenging topics and activities.

## As a Reference

You can use the Concepts sections in this book as a first source for definitions of terms, background information on given topics, and summaries of procedures.

# ICONS SERVE AS CUES:

Throughout the book, you will find icons in the margin representing various kinds of information. These icons serve as at-a-glance reminders of their associated text.

**Topic:**
Represents the beginning of a topic

**Check Your Skills:**
Represents a Check Your Skills practice

**Task:**
Represents the beginning of a task

**Apply Your Knowledge:**
Represents an Apply Your Knowledge activity

**Student Note:**
Highlights information for students

**Glossary Term:**
Represents a definition; this definition also appears in the glossary

**Quick Tip:**
Represents a tip, shortcut, or additional way to do something

**Warning:**
Represents a caution; this note typically provides a solution to a potential problem

**Web Tip:**
Refers you to a Web site where you might find additional information

**Instructor Note:**
In the Instructor's Edition, gives tips for teaching the class

**Overhead:**
In the Instructor's Edition, refers to a PPT slide that the instructor can use in the lesson

**Additional Instructor Note:**
In the Instructor's Edition, refers the instructor to more information in the back of the book

*About This Course* **xvii**

# Error-handling and Debugging

**LESSON 1**

## Overview

In this lesson, you will review some of the most common errors JavaScript programmers make. Then, you will explore the debugging functionality available in Internet Explorer's script debugging utility. Finally, you will use specialized error-handling features in the JavaScript language to detect unanticipated errors in your code as well as definable errors caused by user interaction with your Web pages.

## Objectives

To have the experience of debugging code and handling errors, you will:

**1A** **Detect common coding errors by reviewing blocks of JavaScript code.**

After reviewing some of the most common errors made by JavaScript code developers, you will inspect several blocks of code and be asked to comment on whether they contain coding errors.

**1B** **Interact with commonly-used debugging features in Internet Explorer's script debugger.**

You will enable and turn on the script debugger, use its tools to step through code, set and clear breakpoints, and use the Command window to check data values as code is processed. You will also use the Call Stack window to examine program threading, and use the Running Documents window to view open files in a frameset document.

**1C** **Use the JavaScript language to capture and handle errors.**

You will use the try...catch construct to capture and display information about coding errors, create custom error messages with the `throw` clause in response to user interaction, and nest try...catch constructs to handle different categories of errors effectively.

**Data Files**
err.html
err2.html
timestable.html
stepping.html
DTProject.html
DTLeft.html
DTRight.html
zodiac.js
birthstones.js
blank.html
tc2.html

**Lesson Time**
1 hour, 30 minutes

# Topic 1A

## Common Scripting Errors

Here's a list of some of the most common coding errors made by JavaScript developers:

- Using variables that aren't defined.
- Ignoring letter casing.
- Unbalanced brackets.
- Unbalanced parentheses.
- Omitting the concatenation symbol.
- Using one equals sign in places where two are needed.
- Mixing up properties and methods.

Going through examples of each type of error should help you to "develop" an eye for catching them as you code.

### Using Variables That Aren't Defined

As a JavaScript programmer, you might be aware of the forgiving nature of the language when it comes to creating and using variables—instead of having to explicitly create variable names for later use, you can create them on the fly. However, that doesn't mean you can forget about *when* the variables you use are defined in code:

```
alert(message);

...bunch of code...

var message = "Hello world!";

...more code...
```

In the example above, the variable `message` is used by the Window object's `alert()` method before it is defined and assigned a string value. When processed, this code would halt processing and cause an error dialog box to appear.

At this point you might wonder: "But what about all those function definitions at the beginning of the <HEAD> section that use variables that aren't defined until further down the page?" The answer is that although functions are among the first parts of a Web page loaded by the JavaScript interpreter, they are not actually run until they are called. So, the crux of the matter with regard to defining variables before using them is that you have to pay attention to their use within a given level (scope) of the code as it is processed.

Another particularly difficult-to-detect situation in using undefined variable names often occurs when you code functions:

```
function scoreQuiz(numOfAnswrs, correctAnswers, timeTaken)
  {
  bonusPts = 100 * (120 - timeTaken);
  score = correctAnswers/numOfAnswers * 100 + bonusPts
  return score;
  }
```

Note that the first parameter passed to the function, numOfAnswrs, differs from numOfAnswers, the name used in the code block within the function. This difference causes the JavaScript interpreter to consider numOfAnswers to be the undefined variable, because it differs from its correctly passed, yet incorrectly spelled cousin in the arguments list. Thus, the runtime error dialog box will misleadingly show the line number containing numOfAnswers to be the cause of the error, not the line containing numOfAnswrs—a subtle (and sometimes frustrating) situation.

## Ignoring Letter Casing

It's commonly known that JavaScript is a case-sensitive scripting language that throws errors when developers use incorrect letter casing. What you might not realize is that, depending on what is incorrectly cased, the browsers' runtime error reporting differs significantly.

Take the following code block, for instance:

```
var ST = "nj";
If(ST == "Nj")
  {
  fixedST = ST.toUppercase();
  alert(fixedST);
  }
```

In it, you will find three casing errors:

- *Using* If *instead of* if. JavaScript recognizes the if language component only when it is entirely in lowercase. Thus, the uppercase I causes the interpreter to throw cryptic runtime error messages:
  - In IE, the message *Object expected* is shown.
  - In NN, the message *If is not defined* is shown.
- *Using incorrect logic.* Because JavaScript recognizes nj, Nj, and nJ as three distinct entities, the if statement would end up fixing only one of the three possible incorrectly-cased state abbreviations. Although this situation does not cause an error message to appear, its incomplete logic catches the problem only some of the time.
- *Using incorrect casing in a method or property name.* JavaScript object and property names are case-sensitive and will not function unless coded correctly. Thus, ST.toUppercase() should be ST.toUpperCase(). Both browsers provide error messages that point you toward fixing the method or property, but your first guess might be that you were mistaken that the property or method existed, rather than that you incorrectly typed it:
  - In IE, the message *Object doesn't support this property or method* is shown.
  - In NN, the message *ST.toUppercase is not a function* is shown.

## Unbalanced Brackets

Many programming constructs in JavaScript use a pair of curly brackets ( { } ) to enclose a series of statements within them. Accidentally leaving off a bracket or two can be frustrating to locate, as the following example of a function definition shows:

```
function someFunc()
{
var a = 1;
var b = 2;
if(b >= a)
{
if(b != a)
{
alert("b is bigger.");
}
else
{
alert("b equals a.");
}
}
```

Taking the time to format the code block enables you to more easily locate the error:

```
function someFunc()
  {
  var a = 1;
  var b = 2;
  if(b >= a)
    {
    if(b != a)
      {
      alert("b is bigger.");
      }
    else
      {
      alert("b equals a.");
      }
    }
```

In this example, which is identical to the first except for a little formatting, you can more easily see that the closing bracket for the function is missing.

## Unbalanced Parentheses

Similar to the problem of unbalanced brackets, detecting unbalanced parentheses is thorny—and more difficult, given the lack of an approach to formatting code in such a way as to make them easy to detect. Take the following example:

```
if(monSalary + 150)/monSalary > 1.1)
```

At first glance, you might think that the parentheses around the numerator to add `150` to `monSal` before comparing it to `1.1` are OK, but what's missing is the initial, almost redundant-looking opening parenthesis to wrap the entire expression within the `if` construct. Unfortunately, the best approach to finding whether the opening or closing brackets are out of kilter is to take a code block, scan it to count up the number of times you use each parenthesis symbol, and then start looking for whether you have one too few or one too many. It's tedious, but productive.

## Omitting the Concatenation Symbol

In situations where you might send dynamic messages back to the user based on his or her interaction and input with a Web page, you will often work with code that uses a combination of string variables and primitive string values (not to mention escape characters). With all that going on, chances are that you might occasionally miss hooking things up appropriately with the concatenation operator, and then be faced with trying to find the needle in the haystack:

```
alert("Dear " + name + ":\n\n" + "You have answered " +
numCorrect + "questions correctly,\n\n" "but you missed the
following questions:\n\n" + QNumWrong_Array +".\n\n" + "You did
not score a passing grade, and will\n\n" + "have to take the
test again. It's schedule for\n\n" + nextTestDate);
```

You might set up a convention that enables you to format long messages to improve readability and error detection:

```
alert("Dear " + name + ":\n\n" +
    "You have answered " + numCorrect + ⇒
    "questions correctly,\n\n" +
    "but you missed the following questions:\n\n" +
    QNumWrong_Array + "\n\n" +
    "You did not score a passing grade, and will\n\n" +
    "have to take the test again. It's scheduled for\n\n" +
    nextTestDate);
```

*Because of the limited margin of the page, the ⇒ symbol indicates that the next line would otherwise proceed on the same line.*

Note that the end of each line displays at least one escape character and concatenation operator. (The third printed line contains the error.)

## Using One Equals Sign in Places Where Two Are Needed

JavaScript's distinction between the assignment operator ( = ) and comparison operator ( == ) can often lead you astray as you craft comparisons in `if` constructs and loops. Take, for example, the following code block:

```
var x = 2;
if(x = 10)
  {
  alert(x);
  }
```

At first glance, you might think that the alert box will not be displayed because `x` equals 2, not 10. Think again. Because the expression inside the `if` statement is an assignment, not a comparison, the value 10 will always be assigned into `x` and will always make the `if` statement `true`, no matter what value you assign in `x` beforehand.

This error is especially annoying to find because it's subtle, doesn't show up in an error dialog box, and is detectable only when you begin testing your code. That's because it is essentially a logic error that causes the `if` statement to always evaluate as `true`.

## Mixing Up Properties and Methods

Remember that one of the main differences between properties and methods is that properties *are*, whereas methods *do*. In other words, properties are nothing more than values held in special variable names associated with an object, such as `thisString.length`, a numeric value equal to the number of characters of

*Lesson 1: Error-handling and Debugging* **5**

a string stored in the variable `thisString`. By the same token, methods are nothing more than functions that perform tasks on behalf of an object with which they are associated, such as `window.alert("Hello")`, the task of opening an alert box and displaying the word *Hello* in it.

Although the examples above seem very different, there are times when you might mistakenly think of a property as a method, and a method as a property. This is especially true when working with the Date and String objects, whose many methods might seem more like properties. Take the following code block, for instance:

```
var today = new Date();
alert(today.getFullYear);
```

On the face of it, you might think that the Date object just keeps a bunch of properties within it—one being the `FullYear` property—which can be pulled out at any time. But since the Date object is really a numeric value (the number of milliseconds from the time of its instantiation back to a base year), all the values you obtain from it must be calculated (a *doing* activity) and are, therefore, methods. Consequently, `getFullYear` is a method, not a property, which requires that you place parentheses after its name:

```
var today = new Date();
alert(today.getFullYear());
```

Contrastingly, you might reasonably think that the String object's `length` property is a method by using a very logical thought process: "OK, the string gets stored in the variable, so something has to measure the length of the string (a *doing* activity) to come up with a value, right?"

```
var thisString = "Hello world";
alert("The length of the string is: " + thisString.length());
```

Sorry. The creators of JavaScript consider the idea of `length` to be static enough to be a property, not a method:

```
var thisString = "Hello world";
alert("The length of the string is: " + thisString.length);
```

But, changing the contents of a string variable to all upper- or lowercase lettering (with `toUpperCase()` and `toLowerCase()`) is definitely a *doing* activity, requiring parentheses as part of the syntax:

```
var ST = "nj"
alert(ST.toUpperCase());
```

The upshot? Try to keep it all organized, and check reference materials periodically if you get confused.

# TASK 1A-1:
## Reviewing Code Blocks for Scripting Errors

1. Review the following code block:

   ```
   var num = 75;
   if(num = 100)
      {
      alert("The variable num is equal to 100.");
      }
   else
      {
      alert("The variable num is not equal to 100.");
      }
   ```

   **Does it contain an error?**

2. Review the following code block:

   ```
   var today = new Date();
   document.write("<H1>The " + today.getFullYear +
   " Smallville Little League Web Site</H1>");
   ```

   *No parenthesis after the method*

   **Does it contain an error?**

3. Review the following code block:

   ```
   var Name = "Tony";
   var Greeting = "thank-you";
   var Response = "you're welcome";
   document.write(Name + ' said ' + Greeting +
   " to me, to which I replied "
   Response);
   ```

   **Does it contain an error?**

*Lesson 1: Error-handling and Debugging*

4. Review the following code block:

```
function evalThis(a,b,c,d)
{
if(a == 1 || d == 4)
{
alert(a);
if(b == 2)
{
alert(b);
}
if(c == 3)
{
alert(c);
}
}
}
```

Does it contain an error?

5. Review the following code block:

```
function myFunc(sal,month,COLA)
{
  if((sal/month) + COLA) >= 5000)
    {
    document.write("You are not elibible for a ⇒
    COLA this year.")
    }
}
```

Does it contain an error?

# Topic 1B

## Using the Microsoft Windows Script Debugger

*Microsoft Windows Script Debugger* is a debugging utility you can add to your install of Internet Explorer. As of this writing, the installation files are free and downloadable from the Microsoft Web site at:

http://msdn.microsoft.com/downloads/default.asp?url=/downloads/topic.asp?url=/msdn-files/028/001/175/topic.xml

You can also go to Microsoft's Web site (**http://msdn.microsoft.com/scripting**) to access documentation and download information.

Basically, the script debugger is a development environment that enables you to access special tools for locating and fixing errors in your code. The rest of this lesson will step you through the various aspects of the script debugger that are the most useful to your script development needs.

**8** JavaScript: Advanced Programming (Second Edition)

Once installed, the script debugger can be enabled and disabled through the Internet Options dialog box in Internet Explorer.

# TASK 1B-1:

## Enabling Microsoft Window Script Debugger in IE

1. **Open Internet Explorer.**

2. From the main menu, **choose Tools→Internet Options** to display the Internet Options dialog box.

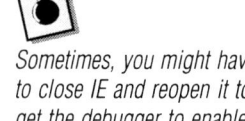

*Sometimes, you might have to close IE and reopen it to get the debugger to enable.*

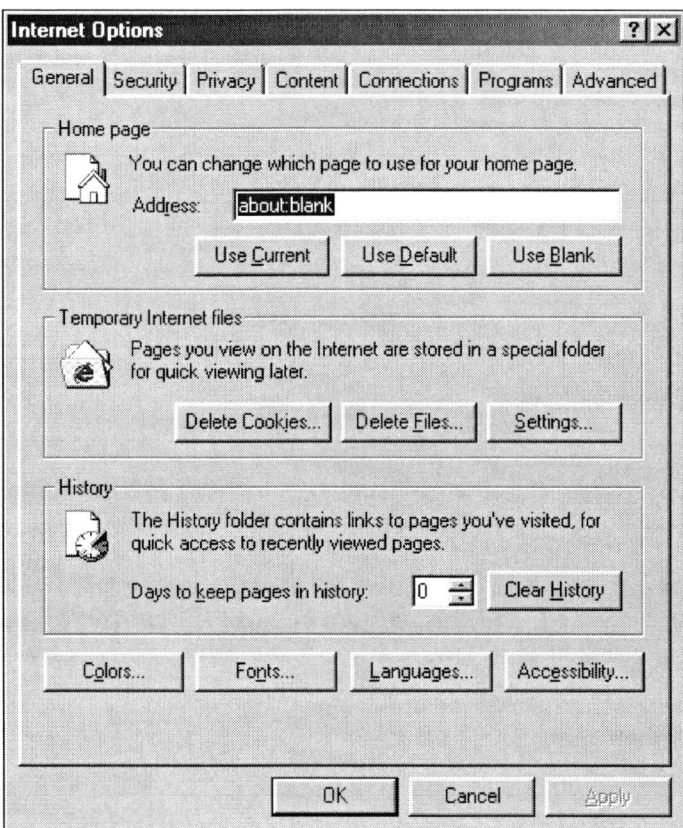

This dialog box enables you to control a wide variety of settings related to your use of Internet Explorer, including security, privacy, content filtering, and default Web services.

Lesson 1: Error-handling and Debugging 9

3. In the Internet Options dialog box, **select the Advanced tab.**

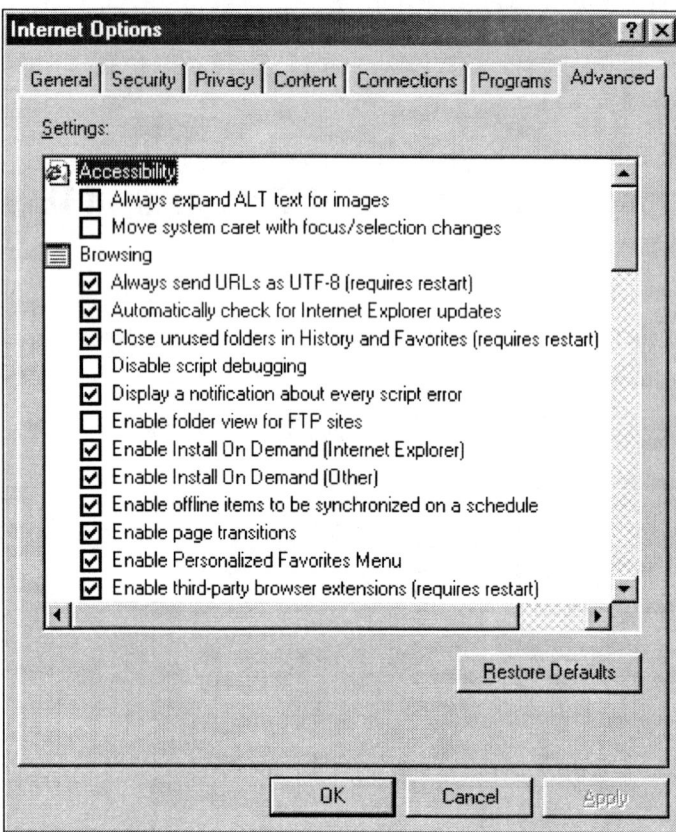

The settings on this tab let you enable and disable much of the browser's functionality.

4. Under the Browsing heading, **verify that the Disable Script Debugging checkbox is not checked, and that Display A Notification About Every Script Error is checked.**

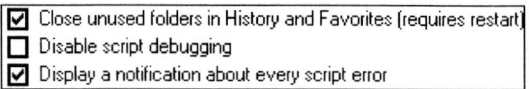

This option is the On-Off switch for Internet Explorer's Script Debugger. By "un-disabling" it, you have set the debugger to activate automatically whenever the browser encounters a scripting error.

5. At the bottom of the dialog box, **click Apply and then OK.** The debugger should now work.

6. In Internet Explorer, from the JavaScript Adv Prog folder, **open the file err.html.**

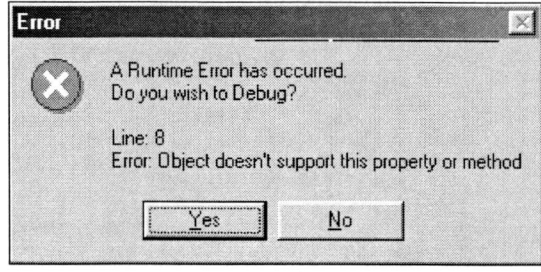

In it, a simple error—a misspelled object name—causes a dialog box to appear, asking you if you would like to debug.

7. **Click Yes** to open the debugger.

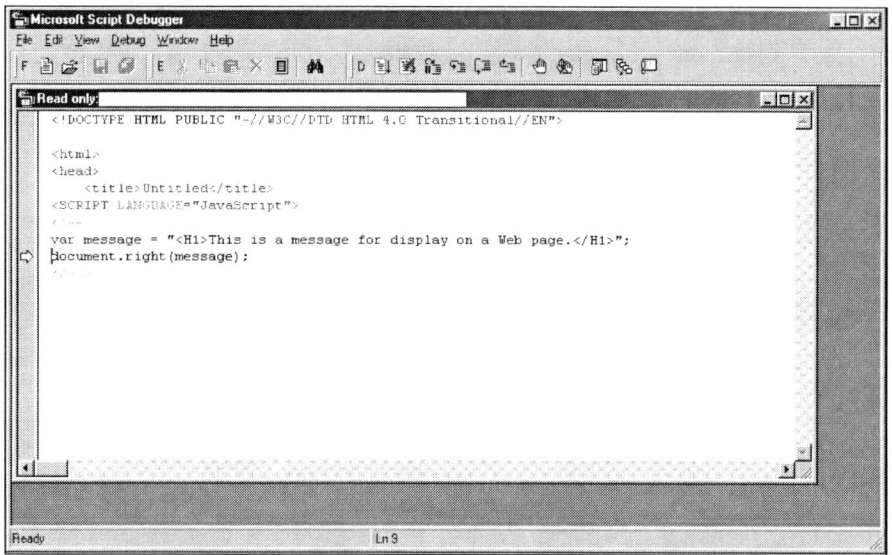

The debugger environment displays the source code of the document being debugged, and highlights the relevant error. In this instance, the word `right` was accidentally typed instead of the word `write`.

Now that you know what to fix, **close the debugger window.**

8. In your text editor, **open err.html and correct the error. Save and test your work** by loading the file in the browser again.

    **Did the debugger find any other errors?**

# CHECK YOUR SKILLS 1-1

### Enabling and Disabling the Debugger

Using the file err2.html, see how Internet Explorer reports errors when you enable and disable the script debugger from the main menu. When you are finished experimenting, make sure the script debugger is enabled before you move on to the next exercise.

**Suggested Time:**
*5 minutes or less*

*You might have to close and reboot IE to apply the new settings.*

### Accessing the Debugger Environment

To turn on the script debugger once it is enabled, you can use three different techniques:

- *Choose View→Script Debugger→Open.* This command opens the debugging environment, irrespective of whether a document is loaded in the browser.

*Lesson 1: Error-handling and Debugging* **11**

- *Choose View→Script Debugger→Break At Next Statement.* This command opens the debugging environment when the JavaScript interpreter attempts to execute the first line of code.
- *Use the* `debugger` *keyword.* This command allows you to open the debugger environment at a specified location in code—namely, the line of your document where you have entered the `debugger` keyword. This feature is useful in that you can use it to skip over blocks of error-free code that must execute before you get to the problem areas you want to debug. In other words, it saves you time and toil in having to step through code that you know already works.

## TASK 1B-2:

### Opening the Debugger

1. In Internet Explorer, **open the file timestable.html.**

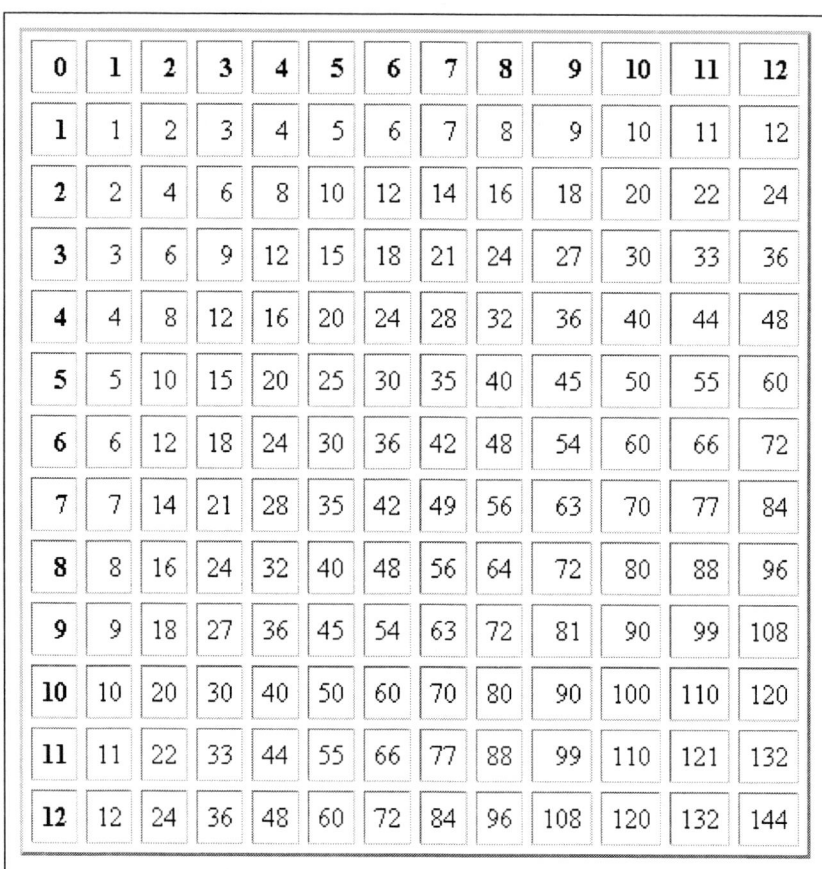

This file successfully generates a times table for the numbers 1 through 12. Because no scripting errors occurred, the debugger did not open.

2. From the main menu, **choose View→Script Debugger→Break At Next Statement.**

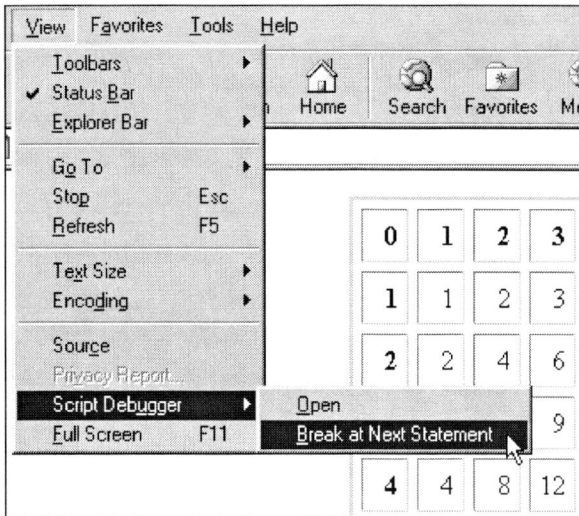

This menu choice directs the browser to open the script debugger as soon as it begins to encounter and interpret JavaScript code.

3. **Refresh the timestable.html document** (press F5).

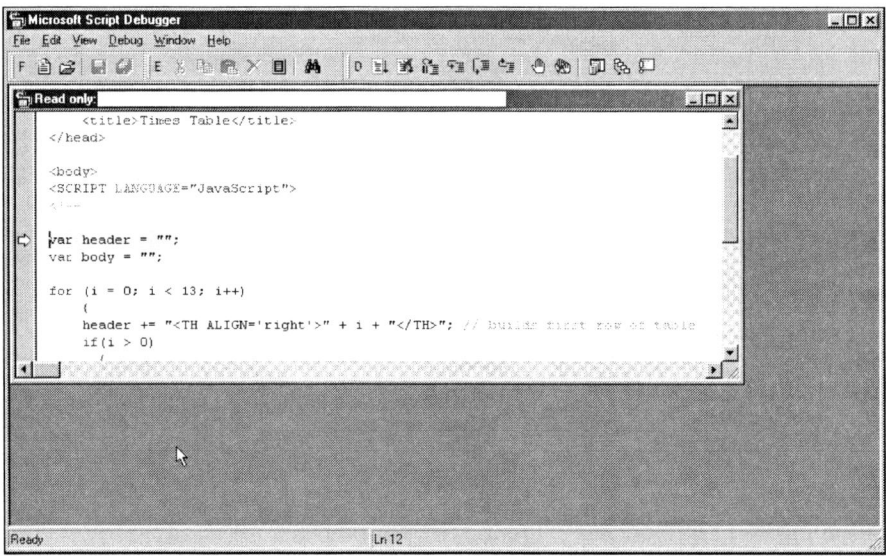

This time, the debugger window opens, highlighting the first line of JavaScript interpreted by the browser (in this case, the declaration statement for the `header` variable.)

4. **Close the debugger window, and then refresh the page again.** This time, the debugger window does not open. Choosing Break At Next Statement is not a permanent setting, but rather a "one shot deal." Once it breaks the execution of your code, it disables itself—you must choose it every time you want to use it to open the debugger.

Now on to the `debugger` keyword.

Lesson 1: Error-handling and Debugging    13

5. In your text editor, **open timestable.html.** Just above the nested j loop, **enter the following code:**

```
debugger
   for (j = 1; j < 13; j++)
     {
     body += "<TD ALIGN='right'>" + (i * j) + "</TD>";
     }
```

6. **Save your work, and then reload timestable.html in Internet Explorer.**

This time, the debugger opens, highlighting the `debugger` keyword at its location in the code.

Unlike the Break At Next Statement menu choice, which stops the execution of your scripts at the first line interpreted, the `debugger` keyword enables you to break code execution at almost any point in your scripting. This flexibility gives you the power of having script execute up to a particular point and then stop, which can often help you determine where things are going wrong when mysterious errors occur.

7. In your editor, **remove the `debugger` keyword from your code, and then save your work. Refresh timestable.html again.** This time, the page loads completely without invoking the script debugger.

**Suggested Time:**
5 minutes

## CHECK YOUR SKILLS 1-2

### Using the debugger Keyword

Using your editor and your browser, try placing the `debugger` keyword at different points in the timestable.html script to see how the script debugger operates.

# Stepping Through Code

The script debugger environment has a set of useful Step Through tools that enable you to step through lines of code to find errors:

| Icon | Name | Toolbar location | Description |
|---|---|---|---|
| | Run | Debugging (D) | Executes the currently highlighted line of code, and then runs all the remaining code, unless stopped by a breakpoint. |
| | Step Into | Debugging (D) | Executes the currently highlighted line of code, and, if applicable, moves into a stacked code construct, such as a code block contained in a function that has been called. |
| | Step Over | Debugging (D) | Executes the currently highlighted line of code, and then moves on to the next line of code at the same level of processing. In other words, it skips over the code in stacked constructs, such as a code block contained in a function that has been called. |
| | Step Out | Debugging (D) | Executes the currently highlighted line of code, and then, if applicable, executes the remaining code in a stacked construct to return to the previous level of processing. For example, it executes the remaining code executed within a function, and highlights the next line of code after the function call. If Step Out is used at the lowest level of processing, it executes all the remaining code, similar to Run. |

At first, the way these Step Through tools operate might seem confusing, because sometimes they appear to do the same thing, and sometimes they operate differently—it's all because of the context in which you use them:

- *Step Out versus Run.* If you press the Step Out button at the "global" level of processing (that is, the level where you would define global variables), it would execute all the remaining code in your document, just like the Run button. But, if you were stepping through a code block held within a function, pressing Step Out would return and stop code execution at the line of code normally executed right after the function call. The Run button always takes you to the end of processing, no matter what context you're in.

- *Step Into versus Step Over.* If you were stepping through code that had no stacked constructs (function calls, and so forth), the behavior of the Step Into and Step Over buttons would appear to be identical. However, introducing function calls would change the situation considerably: the Step Into button would cause you to go to the function definition and step through every single line of code within the function, whereas Step Over would automatically execute the code within the function and take you to the next line after the function call.

## The Command Window

The *Command window* is a blank pop-up window you can open from the Debugging toolbar. It it, you can enter variable names and expressions to determine the values held in them at various points as you step through your code.

For example, say you had a `for` loop that you were stepping through. Each time you went around the loop, the incrementing variable would change by a value of 1. Entering the variable name in the Command window, and then pressing [Enter] as you went around the loop again and again would enable you to see that the value of the variable was changing (or not).

**Command window:**
*A pop-up window, opened from the Debugging toolbar, that enables you to determine the values held in variables as you step through your code.*

The Command window also enables you to test for the existence of variables in a given processing context (see Figure 1-1). If you enter the name of a variable that isn't defined or doesn't exist in the existing processing context, the Command window will display either a blank line or a message stating that no value could be displayed.

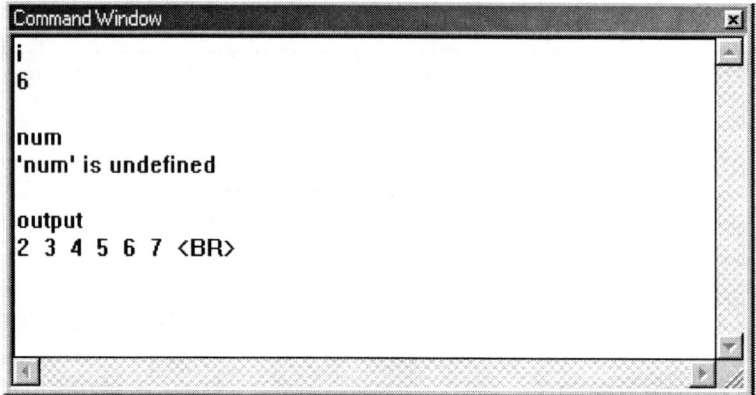

**Figure 1-1:** *The Command window, showing the values of variables during the step-through process.*

# TASK 1B-3:

## Using the Step-through and Command Window Debugging Features

**Objective:** To step through code by using some of the Debugger's Step-through features and the Command window.

1. In your editor, **open the file stepping.html.** It contains three function definitions, three function calls that pass numbers as parameters, and a statement that uses the Document object's `write()` method to display the contents of an output variable.

2. **Locate the `debugger` keyword.** It is placed above the three function calls, and will open the script debugger when the file is viewed in Internet Explorer.

3. In Internet Explorer, **open stepping.html** to activate the script debugger. The debugger highlights the `debugger` keyword, and is ready to undergo the step-through process.

4. **Click the Step Into button once** to see the highlighted area progress through the JavaScript code as it is executed—in this case, it moves off the `debugger` keyword and on to the `addBy()` function call.

5. **Click the Step Into button again.** This time, the highlighted area moves to the beginning of the code block contained in the `addBy()` function—namely, the next line of code to be processed.

6. **Click the Step Into button several more times** to see the debugger move, statement-by-statement, through the loop structure contained in the `addBy()` function.

7. If necessary, from the Debugger toolbar, **click the Command Window button** to open the Command window in the script debugger environment.

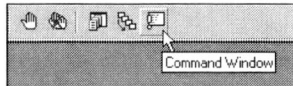

In the Command window, **enter the following variable names** to check their values. (Be sure to press [Enter] after typing each variable name to obtain its value.)

- `i`
- `num`
- `output`

*You don't have to retype the variable names over and over as the loop iterates—just place the insertion point after the variable name and hit [Enter] to obtain new values.*

8. **Use the Step Into button and Command window** to explore how the values of these three variables change as the loop iterates. **Stop clicking the Step Into button** when the highlighted area gets to the `multBy()` function call.

9. With the highlighted area located on the `multBy()` function call, **click the Step Over button** .

   **Did the highlighted area move? Where?**

   **What code (if any) was processed? How can you tell?**

10. **Continue clicking the Step Over button** until the Step Through buttons are grayed out. Then, **close the script debugger window.** You should see the output generated by the three functions.

# CHECK YOUR SKILLS 1-3

**Suggested Time:**
*5 minutes or less*

## More Stepping

Reload stepping.html to continue your exploration of the Step Through buttons to see what they will and will not do. Be sure to use the Step Out button and the Run button to see what differences you can detect in their functionality.

Lesson 1: Error-handling and Debugging

## Breakpoints

Somewhat akin to the `debugger` keyword, *breakpoints* are places in your code where you can stop the execution of code to check variable values in the Command window. Breakpoints are often used in conjunction with the Run button to have code execute up to a given point, and then stop.

**breakpoints:**
*Places in your code where you can stop the execution of code to check variable values.*

To set a breakpoint, place the insertion point at the line of code where you want the debugger to stop, and then click the Toggle Breakpoint button. A reddish highlight will appear on the line, along with a circle in the left gutter. You can set as many breakpoints as you like in your code.

To clear all breakpoints, click the Clear Breakpoints button. If you want to clear a single breakpoint, place your insertion point in the line of code highlighted as a breakpoint and click the Toggle Breakpoint button to remove the red highlighting.

## TASK 1B-4:
### Setting and Clearing Breakpoints

1. In Internet Explorer, **reload stepping.html.**

2. In the debugging window, in the `addBy()` function, **place the insertion point on the following line of code:**

    ```
    output += "<BR>";
    ```

3. From the Debugging toolbar, **click the Toggle Breakpoint button.**

    The button causes a reddish background to appear across the line of code.

    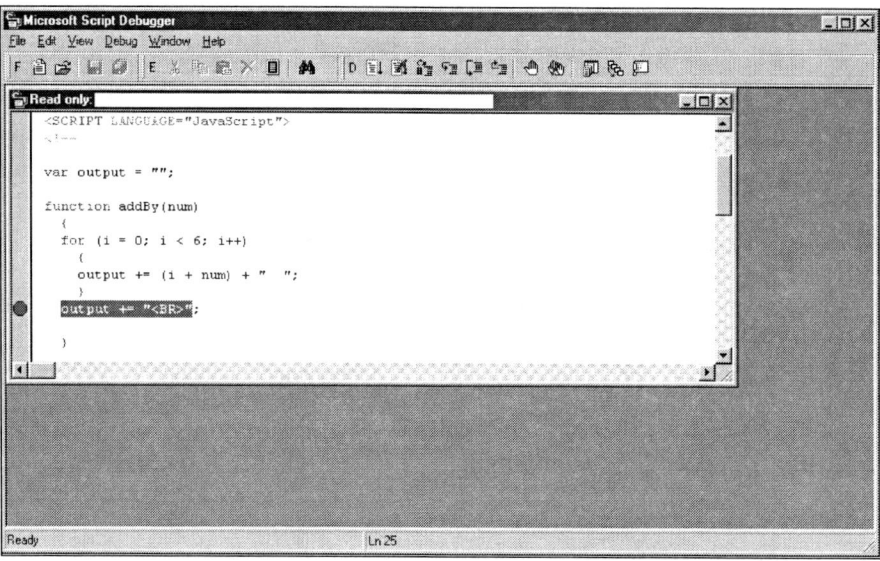

    Note also that a red circle appears in the left gutter. Together, these indications mean that you have inserted a breakpoint at this location in the code.

4. **Press the Toggle Breakpoint button again.** The reddish background and gutter icon disappear.

5. **Toggle the breakpoint on again.** In the other two functions, **locate the identical lines of code and insert breakpoints** there as well. When you've finished, you should have a total of three breakpoints inserted in the functions.

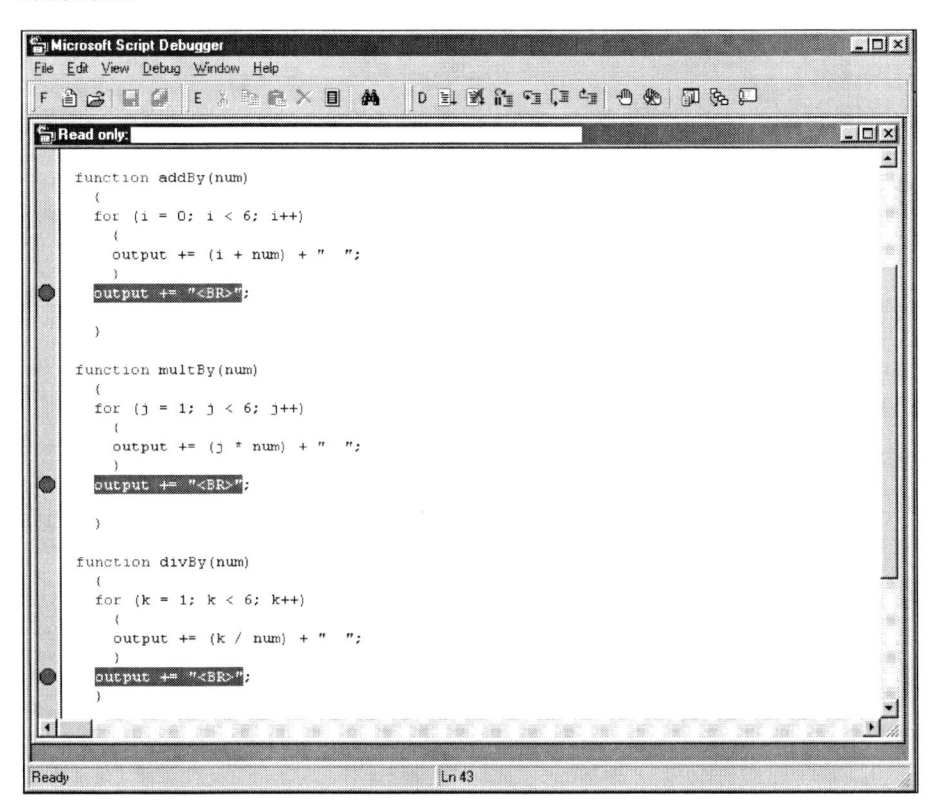

```
function addBy(num)
{
   for (i = 0; i < 6; i++)
   {
      output += (i + num) + " ";
   }
   output += "<BR>";
}

function multBy(num)
{
   for (j = 1; j < 6; j++)
   {
      output += (j * num) + " ";
   }
   output += "<BR>";
}

function divBy(num)
{
   for (k = 1; k < 6; k++)
   {
      output += (k / num) + " ";
   }
   output += "<BR>";
}
```

6. Once you have inserted the breakpoints, **click the Run button.**

You will find that the code stops executing when the debugger encounters its first breakpoint—in this case, the breakpoint contained in `addBy()`.

```
Read only:
<HTML>
<HEAD>
    <TITLE>Untitled</TITLE>
<SCRIPT LANGUAGE="JavaScript">
<!--

var output = "";

function addBy(num)
  {
  for (i = 0; i < 6; i++)
    {
    output += (i + num) + " ";
    }
  output += "<BR>";

  }

function multBy(num)
  {
  for (j = 1; j < 6; j++)
    {
    output += (j * num) + " ";
    }
  output += "<BR>";

  }

function divBy(num)
  {
```

Note that a yellow arrow and background is superimposed over the breakpoint gutter image to show that current processing is halted there.

7. In the Command window, **check the value of the `output` variable, and then answer the following question:**

    **True or False? The line of code marking the breakpoint is executed before processing is stopped by the debugger.**

8. **Click the Run button again** to stop the processing at the second breakpoint. In the Command window, **check the value of `output` again** to see that `multBy()` concatenated a second series of numbers to the string held in it (minus a `<BR>` tag, of course).

9. **Click the Run button again** to get to the third breakpoint, and then **check the value of `output` again** to see the concatenation of the third set of numbers.

10. From the Debugging toolbar, **click the Clear All Breakpoints button.** All the reddish lines and gutter icons for the breakpoints you've set are erased.

11. **Click the Run button again** to complete processing of the page. **Close the script debugger environment** to view the three sets of numbers in the browser window.

## The Call Stack Window

The Call Stack window is a pop-up window you can open from the Debugging toolbar. It indicates the processing context as you step through code.

For example, let's say your code contains functions, which, in turn, call other functions to complete processing. As you step through (and into) these chains of functions, the Call Stack window dynamically changes to indicate the currently-open code constructs. This is especially useful in situations where you might need to figure out whether variables created in one function exist when another is executed—in other words, to examine the relative "global-ness" or "local-ness" of variables.

# TASK 1B-5:
## Viewing the Call Stack in the Call Stack Window

1. In Internet Explorer, **open the file stepping.html.**

2. In the debugging environment, **click the Call Stack button** to open the Call Stack window, if necessary.

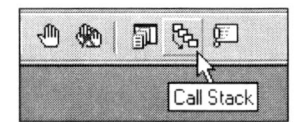

   The window displays a message saying that the browser is currently executing global-level code.

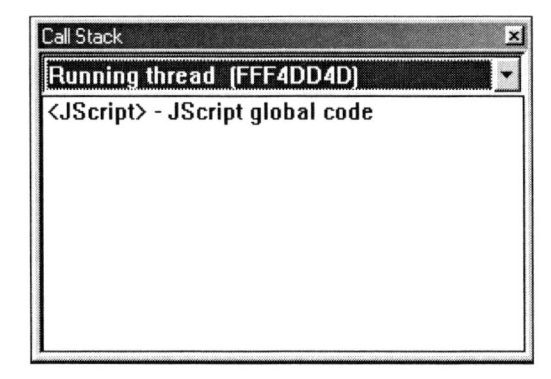

3. Keeping an eye on the Call Stack window as you step through the code, **click the Step Into button several times** to progress, line-by-line, through each of the three function calls. (Use Step Out if you get tired.)

   **What changes did you notice?**

4. In your editor, **move the following function calls:**

Lesson 1: Error-handling and Debugging 21

| Function call: | Move to: |
|---|---|
| `multBy(3);` | The last line of the `addBy()` function. |
| `divBy(4);` | The last line of the `multBy()` function. |

Now the function calls are nested, not called in sequence. Let's see how this plays out in the Call Stack window.

5. **Save and test your work.** As you step through the processing of code, the Call Stack window shows a list of currently processing functions—first the `addBy()`, then the `multBy()`, and then the `divBy()` function—in other words, the function call stack.

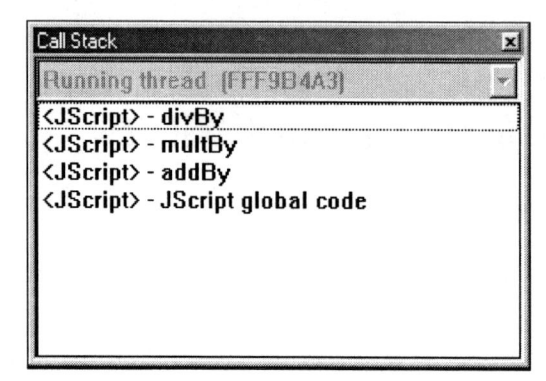

**Can you think of situations where it would be important to view the function call stack while debugging code?**

## The Running Documents Window

The Running Documents window is a pop-up window you can open from the Debugging toolbar. Within it are displayed the instances of Internet Explorer that are currently running, along with the documents currently loaded in them.

If you are working with frameset documents or `<SCRIPT>` includes for `.js` files, this window is useful in that it depicts the open documents in a tree structure to help you see whether the file relationships are how you envisioned them. It also provides a means for you to open code for viewing in the debugging environment. All you have to do is click on the file icon to open its source code window.

# TASK 1B-6:

## Viewing a List of Running Documents

**Objective:** To use the Running Documents window to view a list of documents currently running in Internet Explorer.

1. In Internet Explorer, **open the file DTProject.html.** It is a frameset document that opens the following files:
   - DTLeft.html—an HTML file containing a set of controls that manipulate a data table.
   - DTRight.html—a blank HTML file that receives output from DTLeft.html for display.
   - zodiac.js—a JavaScript include file that contains a data table in the form of an Array object.

2. From the main menu, **choose View→Script Debugger→Open** to open the script debugger environment.

3. From the Debugging toolbar, **click the Running Documents button.**

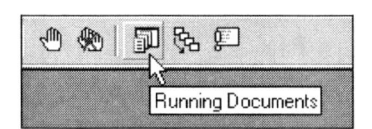

   *Don't worry about how all the code works in this set of documents. You will work with it later.*

   The Running Documents window is displayed. It shows the documents currently running in Internet Explorer by displaying them in a tree configuration.

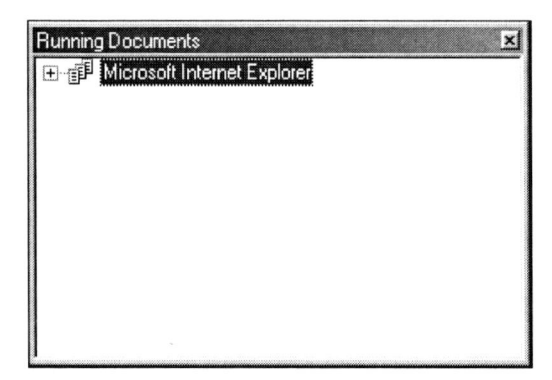

4. In the Running Documents window, **expand the tree** to display all the files.

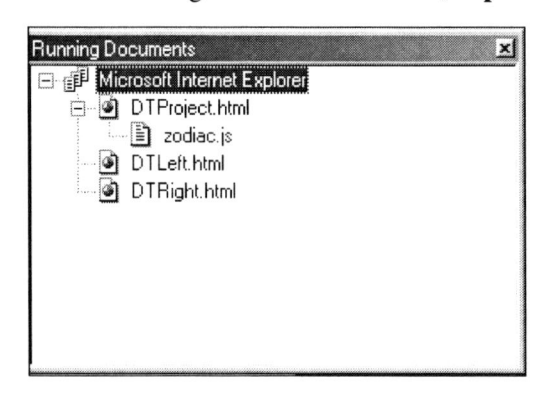

*Lesson 1: Error-handling and Debugging*

Although the JavaScript include file is shown off the DTProject.html file, it is actually included in the DTLeft.html file (an odd anomaly). Let's explore a bit.

5. **Click on each of the four document objects** to open source code windows for them in the debugging environment.

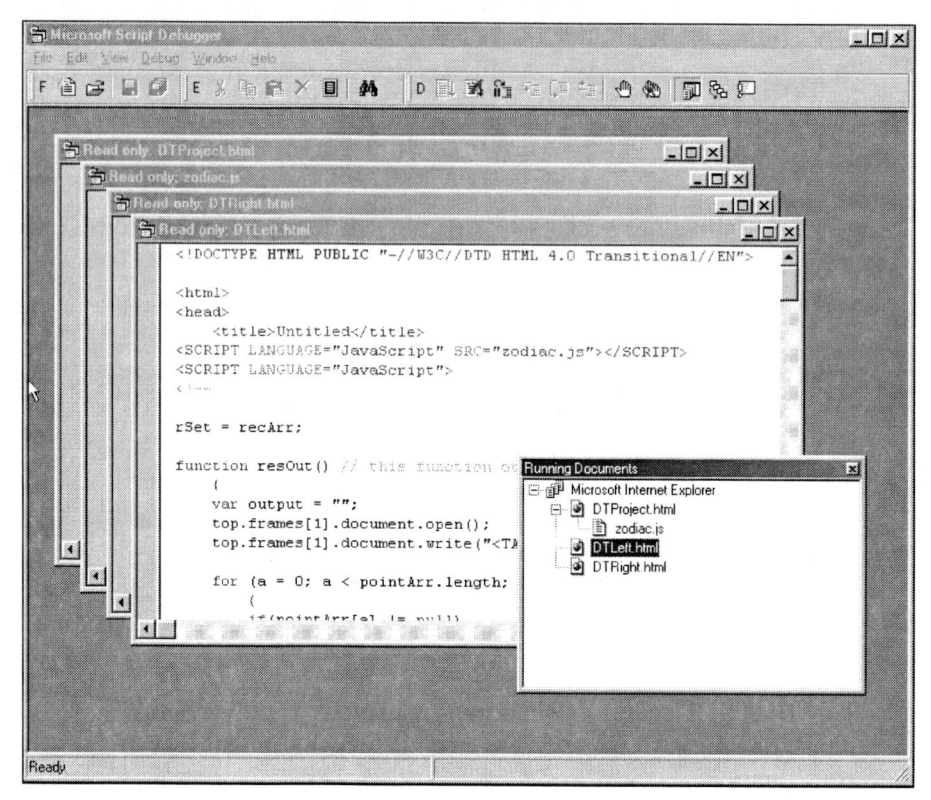

Sure enough, the `<SCRIPT>` include for zodiac.js is in DTLeft.html.

6. **Can you think of situations in which viewing a list of running documents would be useful?**

# Topic 1C

## Language-based Debugging and Error Handling

JavaScript possesses the try...catch coding construct to enable you to check for both expected and unexpected errors in your code so that you can craft error handling features that prevent your pages from "blowing up" on their users. Here's its syntax:

```
try
    {
    ...code to check for errors...
    }
catch(ExObjName)
    {
    ...code to handle errors...
    }
```

To check code for errors, place it within the brackets of the `try` clause. If an error exists within the code, the JavaScript interpreter creates an Exception object, and instantiates it in the variable name you define in the parentheses of the `catch` clause.

The Exception object is a built-in JavaScript object with the following properties:

- In Internet Explorer:
  - `number`—a numeric value describing the specific error as defined by Microsoft in its specification for IE.
  - `description`—a worded message that describes the error in language understandable by a casual user.
- In Netscape Navigator:
  - `name`—a name for the specific type of error as defined by Netscape in its specification of NN.
  - `message`—a worded message that describes the error in language understandable by a casual user.

Note that IE's `description` property is basically the same thing as NN's `message` property. As usual, you must branch code with `if` statements to access these different properties so that yet another layer of error won't occur in your code's ill-fated attempt to access a property that doesn't exist just because the user is using one browser and not the other!

Remember that the try...catch construct is not a panacea—it does not enable you to catch and fix every possible error in your code. Specifically, it does not operate on syntax errors—those very basic errors that occur when you type in the components of the JavaScript language incorrectly.

# TASK 1C-1:

## Coding try...catch Statements

1. In your editor, **open blank.html.** This file is an blank HTML file with empty JavaScript code blocks placed in the <HEAD> section and the <BODY> section. In it, you will code a simple try...catch programming construct.

*Please use single quotes where indicated.*

2. In the `<HEAD>` section, in the empty `<SCRIPT>` block, **enter the following code:**

```
try
  {
  alert('This message brought to you by the try clause.');
  alert('This message too. No errors here!');
  }
catch(ExObj)
  {
  if(ExObj.description)   // tests for IE property
    {
    alert("Ooops! Here's your error IE user: " +
ExObj.description);
    }
  else
    {
    alert("Ooops! Here's your error NN user: " +
ExObj.message);
    }
  }
```

Here's how the code works:

- The `try` clause scrutinizes the code within it for errors that might occur. If none occur, the `catch` statement is ignored.
- On an error within the `try` clause, JavaScript creates an Exception object and assigns it into the `ExObj` variable name. (Note that the variable name used to hold the Exception object can be any valid JavaScript name.)
- The `if` statement tests for the existence of the `description` property to detect whether the user is viewing the page in Internet Explorer:
  — If so, then an alert message using IE's `description` property for the Exception object is displayed.
  — If not, then the `else` clause's alert message using NN's `message` property for the Exception object is displayed.

3. **Save the file as tc1.html, and then load the file in your browser.** The code should run without an error.

4. Let's create an error now. In your editor, in the script you just entered, **modify the following line of code:**

   alert**xxx**('This message too. No errors here!');

*Your changes to the message in the alert statement don't really have anything to do with the actual error.*

You've added bogus characters to the Window object's `alert()` method. Let's see what that does.

5. **Save and test tc1.html in both browsers.** Here's what should happen:
   - Both browsers should successfully display the first alert message in the `try` clause.
   - In IE, the second alert message is directed to the IE user, along with the string value in `ExObj.description`.
   - In NN, the second alert message is directed to the NN user, along with the string value in `ExObj.message`.

26   JavaScript: Advanced Programming (Second Edition)

The second "caught" error messages indicate that JavaScript looked for an object or function named `alertxxx()`, couldn't find one, and threw an exception to the `catch` clause explaining the error. Not all errors are caught in this way, however.

6. Let's create a different kind of error now. In your editor, in the script you entered, **modify the line of code again:**

   alert ('**We've got** errors here!');

   Although you fixed the previous error by removing the xxx's, you've created a new error with the apostrophe in the word *We've* by accidentally closing the single-quote surrounding the string.

7. **Save and test your work in both browsers.** This time, a typical runtime error message (a syntax error) appears in IE; in NN, a blank page loads. Upon opening NN's JavaScript Console, you'll find that it comes across the same error.

   The moral of the story? Syntax errors are detected by the JavaScript compiler before the code is actually executed, so don't expect try...catch constructs to operate on them.

## Throwing Exceptions

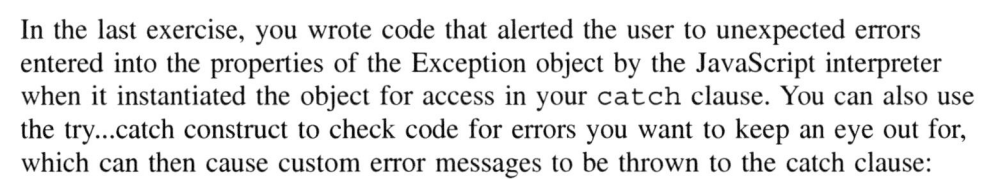

In the last exercise, you wrote code that alerted the user to unexpected errors entered into the properties of the Exception object by the JavaScript interpreter when it instantiated the object for access in your `catch` clause. You can also use the try...catch construct to check code for errors you want to keep an eye out for, which can then cause custom error messages to be thrown to the catch clause:

```
function processTxt(txtbox)
   {
   try
      {
      if(txtbox.value == "")
         throw("You must enter data in the box.");
      }
   catch(excpt)
      {
      alert(excpt);
      }
   ...code that processes txtbox's text...
   }
```

The code block above checks the text (or lack thereof) entered by the user in the text box, and then causes the message *You must enter text in the box* to be thrown to the `catch` clause. Note that the variable `excpt` is used as a plain old string variable—that's right, instead of an Exception object being thrown to it, it receives the string from the `throw` clause.

You can construct multiple throw clauses to check for a variety of errors:

```
function processTxt(txtbox)
  {
  try
    {
    if(txtbox.value == "")
        throw("You must enter data in the box.");
    if(isNaN(txtbox.value))
        throw("Error! Please enter a number in the box.");
    }
  catch(excpt)
    {
    alert(excpt);
    }
  ...code that processes txtbox's text...
  }
```

In the example above, the added code checks to see if the data entered in the text box is a number.

Remember that despite the the existence of custom-thrown messages for the `catch` clause, the JavaScript interpreter still interacts with your code to create an Exception object if necessary. Thus, code branching in the `catch` clause is necessary to detect whether the exception variable is an object or a variable holding a string. This can be done with `if` constructs and the `typeof()` method.

## TASK 1C-2:

### Throwing Custom Exceptions

1. In your browser, **open the file tc2.html.** It displays three drop-down lists, a non-functioning button, and some text that directs the user to make a selection from each box.

2. In your editor, **open tc2.html.** In the `<HEAD>` section, in the blank `<SCRIPT>` block, **enter the following code:**

```
function validate()
  {
  try
    {
    if(frm.SelObj1.selectedIndex == 0)
      throw("0You didn't select from box 1.")
    if(frm.SelObj2.selectedIndex == 0)
      throw("1You didn't select from box 2.")
    if(frm.SelObj3.selectedIndex == 0)
      throw("2You didn't select from box 3.")
    }
  catch(excpt)
    {
    alert(excpt.substr(1));
    frm.elements[excpt.charAt(0)].focus();
    }
  }
```

Here's how the function works:

- In the `try` clause, a series of `if` statements evaluate the `selectedIndex` property of the three Select objects to determine whether the user has interacted with the select lists.
- If the value of `selectedIndex` is zero, then the user hasn't made a required selection. At this point, the `throw` statement throws an exception as a string value to the variable `excpt` in the `catch` clause. In other words, using `throw` creates an intentional error that can then be handled by the `catch` clause.
- Knowing that `excpt` is a string, not an object, the `catch` clause sends `excpt` as an error message to the user in an alert box. Then, using the index number placed in the first character of the string thrown, it gives focus to the select list needing the user's attention.

Let's hook up this function to see how it works.

3. In the `<INPUT>` tag for the Button object, **enter the following code:**

```
<INPUT
 TYPE="button"
 NAME="But1"
 VALUE="Click on Me"
 onClick="validate();">
```

4. **Save and test your work in your browser.** You'll find that, depending on whether you make selections from the drop-down lists, you'll get an error message that directs you to the relevant list box, along with the automatic assignment of focus to the object needing attention.

**Suggested Time:**
*10 minutes*

## Apply Your Knowledge 1-1

### Handling Exceptions

Using information from the previous two tasks, modify the `catch` clause in tc2.html such that it will evaluate unexpected exceptions as objects and as string values from your intentional "errors" thrown in code. Feel free to use such language components as `if`, `else if`, `else`, and `typeof()` to craft your code. Save and test your work by either causing thrown errors to occur or mistyping code (similar to the previous tasks) to invoke the Exception object.

A solution to this exercise is provided in the answer section.

## Summary

In this lesson, you reviewed some of the most common errors JavaScript programmers make. Then, you explored the debugging functionality available in Internet Explorer's script debugging utility. Finally, you used specialized error-handling features in the JavaScript language to detect unanticipated errors in your code as well as definable errors caused by user interaction with your Web pages.

## Lesson Review

**1A** Name some common coding errors made by JavaScript developers.

**1B** List the main features of Internet Explorer's script debugger.




Which did you find most useful?


**1C** Is handling errors with the try...catch construct an either/or proposition (in that you can work only with unexpected errors or define errors with the `throw` clause, but not both)? Why or why not?

YOUR NOTES:

# Custom Objects

## LESSON 2

### Overview

The Document Object Model (DOM) enables you to use a scripting language (such as JavaScript) to control a Web page and its contents. It's like a remote control. When your JavaScript code pushes the buttons (by changing the properties of Document objects, for example), it changes the Web page in some way (even if those changes are behind the scenes). Many pre-defined objects (Document, Form, Frame, and so forth) are provided for you. Sometimes, however, it's helpful to be able to add new objects to the mix. Embedding your JavaScript code within objects can make it easier for you to reuse and share your code with others. In this lesson, you'll learn how to create and use your own custom objects in JavaScript.

**Data Files**
*Default.htm*
*Explore\Objects.htm*
*Lab - Objects\Catalog.js*
*Lab - Objects\CatContent.htm*
*Lab - Objects\CatFrame.htm*

**Lesson Time**
*1 hour, 15 minutes*

## Objectives

To create and use your own JavaScript objects, you will:

**2A** **Use the Object( ) constructor function to create a new object, and assign custom properties to an object.**

You will use the JavaScript Exploratorium to create and analyze simple custom objects.

**2B** **Write a constructor function that initializes an object's properties, and use that constructor function to create an instance of an object.**

You will write constructor functions to create JavaScript objects.

**2C** **Write a constructor function that declares at least one method, and use that constructor function to create an instance of an object.**

You will extend the functionality of objects by writing your own methods.

# Topic 2A

## Introduction to Objects

Custom objects enable you to create complex data structures. You could use custom objects, for example, to create the JavaScript equivalent of a relational database. Custom objects also afford you many of the general benefits of object-oriented programming, enabling you to design your code for reusability and maintainability.

## Properties

From your previous JavaScript programming experience, you should be at least somewhat familiar with the term "object" as it applies to programming. In fact, you've already programmed objects if you've written statements such as the following:

```
window.location = "http://www.elementk.com";
```

This statement assigns a new value to the location *property* of the Window object, effectively changing the Web page that is displayed in the window. You can think of properties as attributes of an object. An object's name, height, width, color—these are its properties. The example above assigned a value ("http://www.elementk.com") to a property. To read the value of a property, you simply move the object/property reference to the right side of the equals sign, like this:

```
currentLocation = window.location;
```

Properties can contain many sorts of values. For example, a property might contain a number, such as 1984 or 3.14159. A property might contain a text string, such as "Big Brother" or "Spencerport Soccer Club." A property might also contain a reference to another object. For example, the property identified by `self.location` returns the Location object for the current window (the window or frame in which the JavaScript code is contained). The Location object contains information about the current location, such as URL, protocol used to load the page, and so forth.

## Methods

In addition to properties, objects may also have associated methods. A *method* is a function that belongs to the object. For example, the Location object has a method called `reload()`, which reloads the window from the current URL.

*property:*
An attribute of an object, such as width, name, and so forth. You can set a property (that is, a value can be assigned to it) and you can get a property (when you read its value).

*method:*
A function that "belongs" to an object.

34  JavaScript: Advanced Programming (Second Edition)

# Events

Objects can respond to various *events*. For example, the HTML statement

```
<INPUT name="btnMT" type="button" value="Empty" onClick=⇒
"doEmpty( )">
```

identifies a JavaScript function—doEmpty()—that should run when the user clicks the Empty button.

Properties, methods, and events are the stuff that JavaScript objects are made of. For the remainder of this lesson, we'll explore how these elements of custom objects are defined and used.

# Creating a Simple Custom Object

The *Object() constructor* function enables you to create a new, empty object. For example, the statement

```
rutabaga = new Object();
```

creates a new object, named rutabaga. The new rutabaga object contains no properties, but you can create a property simply by assigning a value to one. For example,

```
rutabaga.latinName = "Brassica napus";
```

gives rutabaga a new property (latinName) and assigns the new property the value "Brassica napus." Incidentally, this ability to create a new property simply by assigning it a value applies not only to custom objects, but to predefined objects as well. For example, the statement

```
window.currentVeg = rutabaga;
```

gives the Window object a new property, currentVeg. Bear in mind that this property endures only as long as the object (Window, in this case) remains in memory. If the window is refreshed or reloaded, the custom property will be erased.

# Types of Data That Custom Properties Can Contain

You can assign any JavaScript entity to a property, including variables and other objects. For example, consider the following statements:

```
1. function garden() {
2.   this.veggies = new Array();
3. }
4. function veggie(veggieName) {
5.   this.name = veggieName;
6. }
7. myGarden = new garden;
8. myGarden.veggies[0] = new veggie("Kohlrabi");
9. alert( myGarden.veggies[0].name);
```

In this code snippet, line 7 creates myGarden as an instance of the garden object. Garden objects have one property, an array of veggies. Line 8 creates a new veggie object (named "Kohlrabi") and assigns it as the first element of the myGarden.veggies array. If you run this code, the alert box will display "Kohlrabi."

---

**event:**
*An action that causes a function to run. Events are typically instigated by users. For example, an onClick event occurs when a user points at a particular object (by using a mouse) and clicks a mouse button.*

**Object() constructor:**
*A special method (a function belonging to an object) that is used to initialize an object when it is created. Tasks performed by the object constructor include such things as creating properties, assigning initial values to properties, identifying the object's methods, and so forth.*

*Lesson 2: Custom Objects* **35**

# TASK 2A-1:

## Using the Object( ) Constructor to Create an Object

**Objective:** In this task, you'll use the JavaScript Exploratorium to examine how simple objects can be created using JavaScript's Object( ) constructor.

1. **Open Default.htm.** This file will be referred to throught the course by its name—the JavaScript Exploratorium. A list of topics is displayed in its main menu.

2. **Click on the Objects link** to view the page for the Objects topic. (You can return to the list of topics at any time by clicking on the JavaScript Exploratorium link in the upper-left corner of the page.) The Objects page consists of two general areas: the Code Box and the Evaluator. In the Code Box, you will enter JavaScript code to create custom objects. In the Evaluator, you will examine the results of your JavaScript code.

3. In the Evaluator, **change the contents of the Object text box from** *document* **to** *car*, **as shown below, and then press [Enter].**

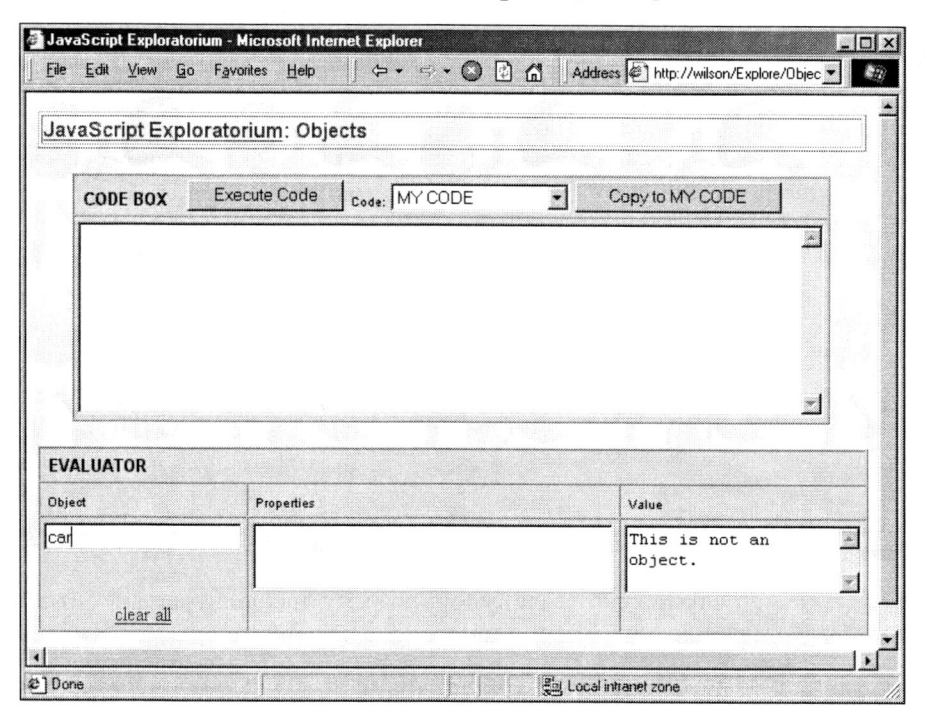

   The Value text box indicates that "car" is not, in fact, an object.

4. In the Code Box, **enter the following, being sure to capitalize letters as shown:**

   ```
   car = new Object();
   ```

5. **Click Execute Code.** If you entered the statement correctly, the Evaluator automatically updates the Properties list, indicating that car is now a valid object, although it doesn't have any properties yet.

36 *JavaScript: Advanced Programming (Second Edition)*

6. Add the statement `car.year = 1999;` as shown below:

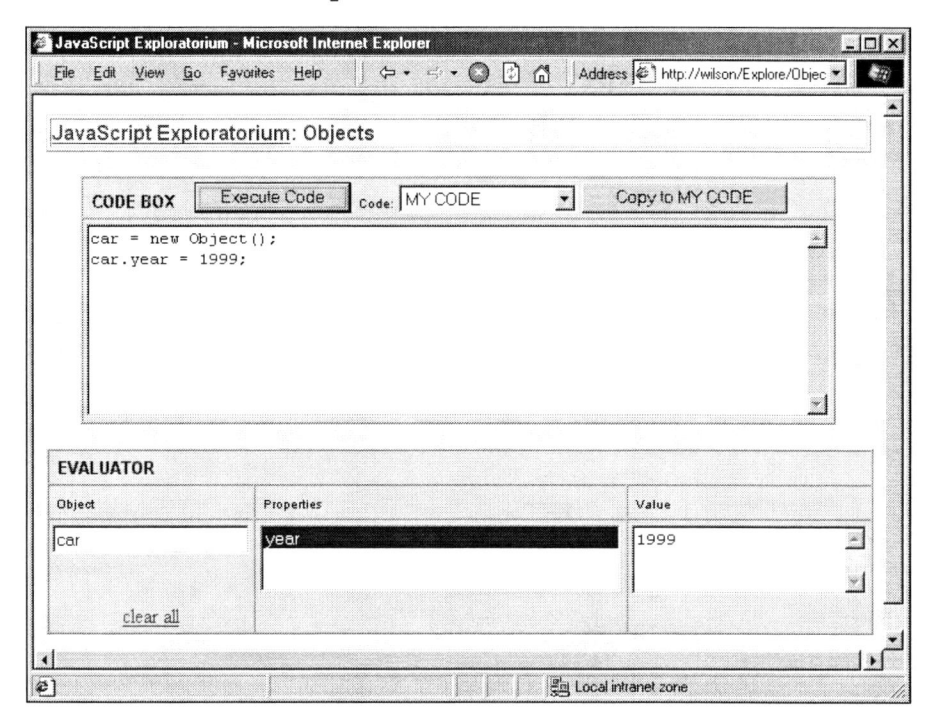

7. **Click Execute Code.** The Properties list for car now shows the year property. Because year is selected, its value, 1999, is displayed in the Value text box.

8. **Add another statement to the Code Box that will add a "make" property to the object, with an initial value of "Ford."** (Hint: Because "Ford" is a text string, it will need to be within quotes.)

9. **Execute the code, and verify that the make property has a value of "Ford."** (Click on "make" in the Properties list.)

10. **Click Clear All.** A dialog box appears, informing you the memory will be cleared of any objects you created. **Click OK.** (The "clear all" link reloads the current page.)

# Topic 2B

## Constructor Functions

As you saw in the previous task, the Object( ) constructor creates an object that has no properties. You can create properties on-the-fly by simply assigning values to them. In most cases, however, you will want objects of a certain type to have a standard set of properties. Of course, you could write a special function to construct the object and define its properties. That, in fact, is what you'll do next.

A constructor function is similar in most regards to any other function. However, JavaScript provides some additional language features that you should know about when writing constructor functions.

- Within the constructor function, the keyword `this` refers to the object that the constructor function creates.

Lesson 2: Custom Objects  37

- The name of the constructor function serves as the object name.
- A function can be defined as a method of an object by assigning the function to a property of the object.

In the tasks that follow, you will examine how to use these features when writing a constructor function.

## TASK 2B-1:

### Creating an Object by Using a Constructor Function

**Setup:** Before you begin this task, make sure that you are viewing the Objects page in the JavaScript Exploratorium.

1. In the Code Box, **enter the following code.** (If you indent in the Code Box, use the Space key, not Tab.)

   ```
   function Car(theMake,theYear){
     this.make = theMake;
     this.year = theYear;
   }
   myCar = new Car("Chevy",1987);
   ```

   *Note the different coding style used in step 1. Many developers use it.*

2. **Type the object name myCar in the Object text box.**

3. **Click Execute Code.** Your code runs, and the Properties list is updated. The make and year properties are shown in the list. **Click on each of the properties** to view its value in the Value text box. (If the myCar object doesn't exist, make sure you capitalized and spelled the object name and the constructor function names correctly.)

4. **Add statements in the Code Box so that it appears as follows.** (The two new statements are shown in bold text.)

   ```
   function Car(theMake,theYear){
     this.make = theMake;
     this.year = theYear;
   }
   myCar = new Car("Chevy",1987);
   myCar.color = "blue";
   yourCar = new Car("Buick",1954);
   ```

5. **Click on Execute Code.** All of the statements in Code Box are executed, and myCar has a new property, color. You can verify that the value of myCar.color is "blue" by selecting "color" in the Properties list.

6. In the Object text box, **change "myCar" to "yourCar" and press [Enter]** to display the properties of yourCar. The yourCar object has the two properties (make and year) that were defined in the Car( ) constructor function, but yourCar does not have a color property because only myCar was assigned a color, outside of the constructor function. As you can see, constructor functions provide an effective way to define an object's minimal set of properties. Furthermore, with constructor functions, initial property settings can be defined when the object is created.

7. **Modify the statements in the Code Box** so that it appears as follows:

```
function Car(theMake,theYear){
  this.make = theMake;
  this.year = theYear;
  theDate = new Date();
  this.objectBorn = theDate.toLocaleString();
}
myCar = new Car("Chevy",1987);
myCar.color = "blue";
yourCar = new Car("Buick",1954);
```

8. **Click on Execute Code, then use the Evaluator box** to view the objectBorn properties of the myCar and yourCar objects. The objectBorn property contains the date and time that each of these objects was created. As this task illustrated, constructor functions can assign properties using values other than those provided as arguments.

9. **Click Clear All and click OK** to clear all objects from memory and empty the Code Box.

# CHECK YOUR SKILLS 2-1

*Suggested Time: 5 minutes*

## Creating More Custom Objects

1. In the Code Box, enter code for a constructor function that will create a catalogItem object. This object represents a single item in an online catalog. The object should have three properties: the stock number, the name of the item, and the item's price. Create two instances of the catalogItem, to represent items of your own choosing. Use the Evaluator to verify that the objects have been created.

2. Above the Code Box is the Code drop-down list. From that list, you can select "Catalog Item Object" to view one way in which this practice task could have been solved. Compare it to your own solution, which you can view again by selecting "MY CODE" from the list.

3. Clear all objects and empty the Code Box. (Use the "clear all" link.)

# Topic 2C

## Methods

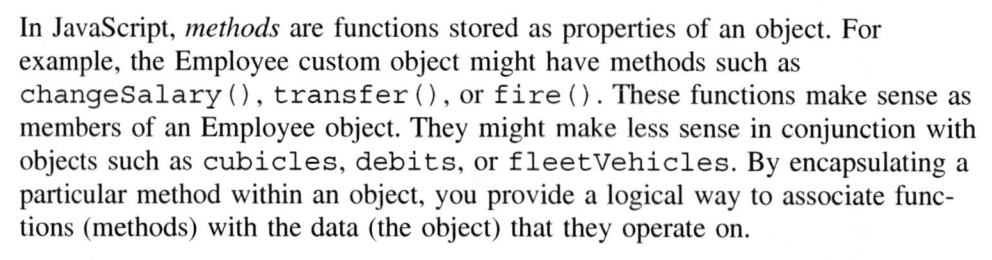

In JavaScript, *methods* are functions stored as properties of an object. For example, the Employee custom object might have methods such as `changeSalary()`, `transfer()`, or `fire()`. These functions make sense as members of an Employee object. They might make less sense in conjunction with objects such as `cubicles`, `debits`, or `fleetVehicles`. By encapsulating a particular method within an object, you provide a logical way to associate functions (methods) with the data (the object) that they operate on.

**methods:**
*Functions stored as properties of an object.*

You declare a method much the same as you would any other function. To associate the function with the object, you assign the function to a property. Examine the code below.

```
1.  function Employee_changeSalary() {
2.    var newSalary = prompt("What is the new salary?⇒
        ",this.salary);
3.    // (Validation routine would go here...)
4.    this.salary = newSalary;
5.  }
6.
7.  function Employee(theName,theHireDate,theSalary) {
8.    this.name         = theName;
9.    this.hireDate     = theHireDate;
10.   this.salary       = theSalary;
11.   this.changeSalary = Employee_changeSalary;⇒
        // Declare method
12. }
```

The `Employee_changeSalary()` function will be a method of the Employee object. Within the `Employee()` constructor function, the `Employee_changeSalary()` function is assigned to the `changeSalary` property. As with constructor functions, in methods, the `this` keyword refers to the object itself.

In line 11, notice that neither the method name, `this.changeSalary`, nor the function reference, `Employee_changeSalary()`, is followed by parentheses. When JavaScript encounters a function name followed by parentheses, it attempts to run that function. When assigning a property to a method name, you do not want to call the function, you want to refer to the function itself.

Given the declarations above, you could create a new employee by using the statement: `employeeX = new Employee("Fred", 1997, 45000);`. Later, you could change the employee's salary with the statement: `employeeX.changeSalary();`

The rules for naming methods are the same as those for any function. However, you might find it beneficial to use a naming scheme like the one used for `Employee_changeSalary`. This approach helps to identify this function as a method, rather than just another run-of-the-mill function. In this scheme, the first part of the function name (before the underscore character) identifies the object to which the method belongs, and the second part identifies the purpose of the function. It is a good habit to make the second half of the function name identical to the name you assign to the property that holds the method.

40   JavaScript: Advanced Programming (Second Edition)

Typically, you assign a function to an object property within a constructor function. However, you could make the assignment outside of the constructor, and you could even assign a new method to predefined objects, such as Window.

The previous example illustrates how methods are typically declared. Because the `Employee_changeSalary()` function is declared outside the Employee constructor function, `Employee_changeSalary()` could be shared with other objects. If you wanted to, you could declare it inside of the `Employee()` constructor function, like this:

```
1.  function Employee(theName,theHireDate,theSalary) {
2.    function Employee_changeSalary() {
3.      var newSalary = prompt("What is the new salary?⇒
              ", this.salary);
4.      // (Validate here...)
5.      this.salary = newSalary;
6.    }
7.    this.name          = theName;
8.    this.hireDate      = theHireDate;
9.    this.salary        = theSalary;
10.   this.changeSalary  = Employee_changeSalary;⇒
              // Declare method
11. }
```

As ugly as it is, this approach declares the `Employee_changeSalary()` function so that its scope is local to the `Employee()` constructor function.

# TASK 2C-1:

## Adding Methods to Objects

**Setup:** Before you begin this task, make sure that you are viewing the Objects page in the JavaScript Exploratorium.

1. In the Code drop-down list, **select Car Object and execute the code.**

2. **Enter *bigCar* in the Object text box and press [Enter]** to refresh the Properties list.

3. **Select each of the properties in the Properties list box, and view its value in the Value text box.** In the following steps, you will add a method that will calculate miles per gallon, based on the miles and gallons properties of the Car object.

4. **Modify the code in the Code Box as shown below:**

    ```
    function Car_mpg () {  return Math.round(this.miles / this.gallons);}
    function Car(theMake,theYear,theMiles,theGallons) {
      this.make = theMake;
      this.year = theYear;
      this.miles = theMiles;
      this.gallons = theGallons;
      this.mpg = Car_mpg;
    }
    bigCar = new Car("Mercury",1967,540,41);
    alert("This big car gets " + bigCar.mpg() + " mpg.");
    ```

5. **Execute the code.** An alert box displays the car's gas mileage, rounded to the nearest integer. **Click OK.**

6. **Observe that the call to the mpg method (in the last line of code) includes parentheses after mpg.** To call a function, it is necessary to include the parentheses. Methods are like other functions in this regard. (It also helps you distinguish between properties and methods when you're reading code.)

7. In the Properties list, **select mpg** to display the value of the mpg property. The mpg property contains the Car_mpg function.

8. **Click Clear All** to clear all objects and all code from the Objects page.

**Suggested Time:** *5 minutes*

# CHECK YOUR SKILLS 2-2

## Adding a Method to an Object

1. In the Code drop-down list, select Catalog Item Object. Click on Copy to MY CODE to copy this to your code view. (The Code drop-down list should now show "MY CODE.")

2. Add a tax( ) method that will calculate the sales tax on an item. The sales tax is 8.5%.

3. From the Code drop-down list, you can select "Sales Tax Method" to view one way in which this practice task could have been solved. Compare it to your own solution, which you can view again by selecting "MY CODE" from the list. When you are done, clear all objects and all code from the Objects page.

**Suggested Time:** *45 minutes*

# Apply Your Knowledge 2-1

## Writing Object Constructor Functions

In this activity, you'll finish implementing two objects that represent entries in an online product catalog. You can view an example of the online catalog by clicking on "Lost Mine Web Site Demo" at the JavaScript Exploratorium main menu.

You will implement only the part of the catalog that lists the items. A finished version of the project is in the JavaScript Adv Prog folder, in the Lab - Objects folder. To view the functionality that you are going to implement, open Finished CatFrame.htm in your browser. At this point, the page simply lists the catalog items.

You'll need to write constructor functions for two objects: entry and catalog. The entry object represents a single product entry within the catalog. The catalog object represents the catalog itself. All of the methods for both of these objects have already been written for you. You simply need to declare them in your constructor functions.

42  *JavaScript: Advanced Programming (Second Edition)*

Following is a listing of the code for the files that you'll need to work in. Catalog.js contains the JavaScript code that declares the objects and their methods. In this file you'll need to write constructor functions for the entry and catalog objects. The two areas where you'll need to add code are highlighted in the listing below.

```
/************************************************************
CATALOG.JS contains declarations for the catalog objects.
Objects declared include:
  - entry:   a single product.
  - catalog: contains entry objects.
************************************************************/

/************************************************************
entry object
************************************************************/
// entry constructor function
// NOTE: Put constructor function for entry here.
//       Parameters are thePartID, theItemName, theImage,
//       theDescription, thePrice.
//       Object has one method, buy(). This is declared below.

// entry_buy adds this item to shopping list stored in cookie
function entry_buy() {
    alert("If this feature were finished, you would have just⇒
 added "+ this.name + " to your shopping cart.");
}

/************************************************************
catalog object
************************************************************/
// catalog constructor function
// NOTE: Put constructor function for catalog here.
//       The constructor function takes no parameters.
//       Object has two methods, addEntry() and display()
//       The methods are declared below.

// catalog_addEntry adds an item to the catalog
function catalog_addEntry (entryID, entryName, entryImage,⇒
 entryDescription, entryPrice) {
    this.numberEntries += 1;
    this.entries[this.numberEntries-1] = new entry(entryID,⇒
    entryName, entryImage, entryDescription, entryPrice);
}

// catalog_display writes catalog entries to a table
function catalog_display () {
    // Start a table to display the catalog.
    document.write( '<table width="100%" border="1">' );
    // Get a reference to each entry
    for (var i = 0; i <= this.numberEntries-1; i++) {
        var my = this.entries[i];
        // Start a new row for this entry
        document.write( '<tr align="left" valign="top">');
        // Start a new column for the product image
        document.write( '<td width="160" align="center">');
        // If there is an image, show it. Otherwise,
        // say that there isn't one.
        if (my.picFile > "") {
            document.write( '<img name="' +  my.ID +'" ' );
```

Lesson 2: Custom Objects   43

```
                    document.write( 'src="Images/' + my.picFile + '" ' );
                    document.write( 'width="120" height="120">');
                } else {
                    document.write( '<br><p align="center">⇒
                        <font size="-1">' );
                    document.write( 'Picture not available.</font>' );
                }
                // Create "buy" link. Switch to animated gif on rollover.
                document.write( '<a href="javascript:Catalog.entries⇒
                    ['+ i +'].buy()">' );
                document.write( '<br><font size="-1">⇒
                    Add to Cart</font>' );
                document.write( '</a>' );
                document.write( '</td>');
                document.write( '<td>');
                document.write( '<p><b>' + my.ID + ' ' +⇒
                    my.name + '</b>' );
                document.write( '<font size="-1"> $' + my.price +⇒
                    '</p></font>' );
                document.write( '<p>' + my.description + '</p>' );
                document.write( '</td> </tr>' );
            }
        document.write( '</table>' );
    }
```

Whereas Catalog.js contains code that declares the constructor functions for the catalog objects, CatContent.htm (listed below) actually uses those objects. In CatContent.htm you'll need to write a statement to create an instance of the catalog object, which you will name "Catalog." You'll also need to make a call to the Catalog object's display( ) method, where the product listing should appear in the page. The areas where you'll need to add code are highlighted in the listing:

```
<html>
<head>
<title>Catalog</title>
<meta http-equiv="Content-Type"
        content="text/html; charset=iso-8859-1">
</head>

<body bgcolor="#ffffff" background="Images/mapskchc.gif"
        bgproperties="fixed">

<!-- catalog.js contains declarations for
    the catalog and entry objects -->

<script language="JavaScript" src="catalog.js"></script>

<script language="JavaScript"><!--

// Create an instance of the catalog object
// NOTE: Write a statement here to create a new
// catalog object named "Catalog."
//       (Make sure you capitalize the "C" in "Catalog")
// Stuff entries into catalog object
Catalog.addEntry
  ("SU-200",
  "Sullivan Panning Kit",
  "Pans.gif",
  "This complete kit contains Sullivan's patented stainless⇒
  steel Nugget Finder pans, a sturdy stainless steel classifier⇒
  (made to fit a 5-gallon bucket), a plastic snuffer, and⇒
```

```
  instructions for use. Rugged enough for professional⇒
  panning, yet handsome enough to put on the dinner table⇒
  for unexpected guests.", 99.95);

//     [ ENTRIES OMITTED FOR THE SAKE OF BREVITY ]

Catalog.addEntry
   ("SU-1000",
   "Goose Neck Oil Can",
   "Oilcan.gif",
   "Keep your Sullivan Sluice-o-matic well oiled.⇒
  This oil can has a kink in its neck so you won't get one⇒
  in yours when you oil those hard-to-reach places. Made of⇒
  stainless steel to last a lifetime.", 15.95);

// Write the display out to the page
// NOTE: Create a statement here to display the
// Catalog in a table. Use Catalog's display() method.

//-->
</script>

</body>
</html>
```

1. In your text editor, open Catalog.js and write the two constructor functions that create the objects described on the next page (catalog and entry). If you need help, refer to the finished code in Finished Catalog.js.

   Note that the catalog constructor function will take no parameter, whereas the entry object will take five parameters. The tables below also show what initializations you will need to perform in the constructor functions.

   ---

   **catalog**

   **Parameters:**
   (no parameters)

   **Members of catalog:**
   numberEntries ........ initially 0
   entries .................... initially contains a new, empty Array object
                                         (eventually the array will hold entry objects)
   addEntry (method).. Refers to function catalog_addEntry
   display (method) ..... Refers to function catalog_display

   ---

   **entry**

   **Parameters:**
   thePartID
   theItemName
   theImage
   theDescription
   thePrice

   **Members of entry:**
   ID ........................... initially assigned the value of thePartID parameter
   name ..................... initially assigned the value of theItemName parameter
   picFile ................... initially assigned the value of theImage parameter
   description ............. initially assigned the value of theDescription parameter
   price ...................... initially assigned the value of thePrice parameter
   buy (method) ......... Refers to function entry_buy( )

   ---

2. Open CatContent.htm and add the two statements that create the Catalog object and display the catalog. (These statements were described at the beginning of this lab.) Place the statements where they are called for in the code listing.

3. Open CatFrame.htm in your Web browser to verify that the catalog is created and displayed. "CatFrame.htm" should work the same as "Finished CatFrame.htm." If you simply cannot get your project to work correctly, compare your files to the finished files that have been provided for you (Finished Catalog.js, Finished CatFrame.htm, and Finished CatContent.htm).

## Summary

In this lesson, you added to the objects provided by the DOM by creating your own custom objects, including constructor functions and methods.

# Lesson Review

**2A** Write a statement that uses the `Object()` constructor function to create an object named `myNewObject`.

**2B** Write an object constructor function called `Rock` that accepts no arguments and creates an object with three properties—type, origin, and weight—each of which is initialized to contain the string value "not known." Also write a statement to create an instance of the Rock object called "aNewRock."

**2C** Write a statement that you would use to declare a method called `calcDensity()` within an object constructor function. The calcDensity method refers to a function named `Rock_calcDensity()`.

*Lesson 2: Custom Objects* 47

YOUR NOTES:

# Arrays

## LESSON 3

## Overview

JavaScript provides two kinds of generic data structures: objects and arrays. These two types of structures are extremely versatile, especially when used in combination. It is essential to learn how to manipulate arrays in JavaScript, because so much of JavaScript's objects and functionality rely on them. Arrays and objects are closely interrelated in JavaScript. In this lesson, you will learn how to create and use arrays in JavaScript.

### Data Files
*Default.htm*
*Explore\Arrays\Arframe.htm*
*Lab - Arrays\Solution\Matrix.htm*
*Lab - Arrays\Matrix.htm*
*Lab - Arrays\matrix.js*

### Lesson Time
*1 hour, 30 minutes*

## Objectives

To create and use arrays, you will:

**3A** **Explain why it is beneficial to place data within array structures.**

This topic introduces JavaScript arrays. You will identify ways in which arrays can be used. You will also learn how arrays are created and populated with data.

**3B** **Write a custom object constructor function to implement an array, use the Array constructor to create an array, and write a statement to populate an array as you create it.**

You will examine how an object can be used to simplify the creation and management of arrays.

**3C** **Delete array elements and destroy an array.**

You will learn how to delete array elements. You will write a method to remove elements from an array. You will also learn how to destroy an entire array.

**3D** **Write code to implement a multi-dimensional array.**

In this topic, you will learn how to create multi-dimensional arrays. You will create a matrix custom object to simplify the task of working with multi-dimensional arrays.

# Topic 3A

## Introduction to Arrays

A JavaScript *array* is a list or collection of variables, called elements, that are identified by a shared name. Each element in the array can hold any valid JavaScript data type. You refer to a specific element by an index. The elements are numbered, beginning with 0. For example, if you had an array called addresses, then addresses[2] would return the third address in the array. You store and retrieve values in an array much the same as other variables. For example you could assign an address by using the statement:

```
addresses[2] = "1812 Kuyserville-Byersville Road";
```

Later, you might read back the same address.

```
msg = "Property is located at " + addresses[2];
```

Even if you have not created your own arrays, you may have used one of the predefined arrays included as part of the Document Object Model. These predefined arrays are easy to recognize. They are properties of the JavaScript's predefined objects that have "plural" names, such as document.anchors (an array containing references to each of the hyperlinks within a document), document.applets (an array of references to all of the applets embedded within a document), document.forms (an array of all the Form objects with a document), and so forth.

> **array:**
> A list or collection of variables, called elements, that are identified by a shared name, with specific elements in the array identified by an index value.

## Why Arrays Are Useful

Arrays enable you to create data structures that lend themselves to automatic processing. For example, consider the following:

```
for (i=1; i<addresses.length; i++) {
displayAddress(addresses[i]);
}
```

For as many times as there are addresses in the array (the length property of the array returns the number of elements), this routine calls a function that displays each address. As i is increased with each pass through the loop, the next address in the addresses array is passed to the function. It doesn't matter how many addresses are in the array; this routine will always work.

The following function uses variables to accomplish the same task. However, because the variables are identified by name, this routine will not work if more addresses are added. Furthermore, the code itself grows as addresses are added.

```
displayAddress(address1);
displayAddress(address2);
displayAddress(address3);
displayAddress(address4);
displayAddress(address5);
displayAddress(address6);
displayAddress(address7);
```

Arrays enable you to add data lookup functionality to your Web pages. Although very large databases should probably be stored and processed on a Web server, small databases, such as zip code directories, tax tables, and so forth, are ideal for client-side JavaScript. Providing such functionality right on the Web page can eliminate delays involved with requesting such information from a Web server. You should consider providing lookup functionality through client-side JavaScript if lookups are frequent and the volume of data is small (less than 50 kilobytes or so). Of course, you pay a small price up-front in time required for the page to load, but you can pack a lot of data into 50 kilobytes.

## Working With Arrays

To create and process your own arrays, of course you'll need some sort of data that lends itself to a list or matrix format. You'll also need to know the JavaScript commands that enable you to create and populate arrays, and to add elements to and remove elements from arrays. Often, it's useful to create multiple arrays whose elements are related. We'll examine how to perform all of these tasks in this lesson.

## Creating and Populating Arrays

Sometimes, JavaScript arrays are created empty, and then values are stuffed into the elements of the array over time. This array-stuffing process is called populating an array. Other times, JavaScript arrays are populated as they are created. In such cases, we essentially tell JavaScript to "take this list of data elements, and give me a new array that contains them."

## Changing the Size of Arrays

You may have used arrays in other programming languages, such as BASIC, Pascal, or C. Some programming languages have arrays that are static; once they are given a certain number of elements, elements cannot be added or removed. JavaScript, in its characteristic leniency, permits you to add elements or delete elements at will.

## Multi-dimensional Arrays

Unlike arrays in some other languages, JavaScript arrays are one-dimensional. In other words, an array can contain any number of columns in one row, but it cannot contain multiple rows. (Such a multi-dimensional structure is sometimes called a *matrix*.) You cannot create multi-dimensional arrays in JavaScript, but you can accomplish the same effect by creating multiple one-dimensional arrays and using them together.

***matrix:***
*An array limited to a single row that contains any number of columns.*

## TASK 3A-1:

### Identifying Uses for Arrays

1. **In the space provided below, identify possible uses for arrays. Use the examples:**

2. **Share your ideas from Step 1** with other students and add their ideas to your own.

# Topic 3B

## Creating and Populating Arrays

In JavaScript, objects and arrays are interchangeable in many regards. Objects can have elements (as can arrays) and arrays can have properties (as can objects). For example, consider the following statements:

```
thisArray = new Array();
thisArray[0] = "A";
thisArray[1] = "B";
thisArray[2] = "C";
thisArray.Contents = "Alphabet";
```

These statements create an array with three elements, and then give the array a property called `Contents`. Because JavaScript treats objects and arrays similarly, it is possible to use them interchangeably. A special notation even enables you to access properties as though they were elements. For example,

```
alert (thisArray ["Contents"]);
```

displays the value of the `Contents` property which was assigned earlier.

Usually, properties are kept separate in memory from elements. In most browsers, you do not have to worry about a property overwriting an element. However, with the earliest version of JavaScript (in Navigator 2.0), properties are stored as elements. In that version, properties were added in the position following the last element. If you wrote

```
thisArray = new Array();
thisArray.Contents = "Alphabet";
thisArray[0] = "A";
thisArray[1] = "B";
thisArray[2] = "C";
```

then "Alphabet" would be overwritten with the value "A" because `thisArray.Contents` would be treated as the first element in the array, as well as the `Contents` property. It is important to remember this if you plan to use arrays and you want to support Navigator 2.0.

52  *JavaScript: Advanced Programming (Second Edition)*

## Using Objects to Simulate Arrays

There are several ways to create JavaScript arrays. Some techniques only work in the newer browsers. The first technique that we'll examine works in all versions of JavaScript. The first browsers with JavaScript provided predefined arrays (such as document.forms), but they did not provide a way for programmers to directly create their own custom arrays. Arrays had to be constructed by creating an object that simulated the features of an array. This method still works in the current browsers, so it is a good approach for implementing arrays that work across all browser versions. Let's take a look at this method.

# TASK 3B-1:
## Examining an Object That Simulates an Array

**Objective:** To use the JavaScript Exploratorium to examine how an array can be simulated by using a custom object.

1. At the JavaScript Exploratorium's starting page, **click Arrays.** The Arrays lab demonstrates three different ways to create arrays.

2. **Click on the first example: 1. Using An Object To Simulate An Array**
The code for this example is displayed in the bottom frame, and the results of running the code are displayed in the Results text box. For your convenience, the code is also listed below.

```
1.function customArray(theLength) {
2.   this.length = theLength;
3.   for (i=1; i<=theLength; i++) this[i] = null;
4.   return this;
5.}
6.function makeGarden1 () {
7.   var theResult = "";
8.   var myGarden = new customArray(5);
9.   myGarden[1] = "parsnip";
10.  myGarden[2] = "asparagus";
11.  myGarden[3] = "jerusalem artichoke";
12.  myGarden[4] = "salsify";
13.  myGarden[5] = "golden bantam";
14.  for (i=1; i<=myGarden.length; i++) {
15.     theResult+= i + ". " + myGarden[i] + "\n";
16.  }
17.  theResult += "(" + myGarden.length + " elements long.)";
18.  return theResult;
19.}
```

You might recognize the customArray function (lines 1 through 5) as an object constructor function, which is exactly what it is. Let's see how this constructor function is used to build an array.

Suppose a call were made to the makeGarden1 function. First, theResult is declared in Line 7, and then Line 8 creates an instance of the customArray object, which it names myGarden. The myGarden object is initialized with a length of 5.

Let's examine what happens in the constructor function when the object is created. Line 2 assigns the length property of the new customArray object to 5 (the value passed in as theLength). To initialize the values stored in the array, line 3 uses a loop to assign each of the new elements in the array a null value.

Line 4 passes a reference to the new object back to the calling statement (line 8). Thus, after line 8 runs, myGarden is a new custom object with one property, a length of 5.

Lines 9 through 13 add new elements to the myGarden object by simply assigning them values. Note that the first element (element 0) was skipped. This is a bit different from normal JavaScript arrays, which begin at element 0. The reason for this is that early browsers (such as Navigator 2.0) would already be using element 0—to hold the length property. Of course, you could keep the array's length in a separate variable if beginning at element 0 is an issue, but in many cases, beginning at element 1 is fine. This approach is only necessary when you are trying to support very old browsers. Other arrays you will create later in this lesson will begin at element 0.

Stuffing data into an array is tedious, and consumes many lines of code. Lines 14 through 16 demonstrate how, once you have a populated array, you can automatically access all of the elements in an array using a `for` loop. This loop adds each element in the array to the result string, which is returned to the caller in line 18. You can view the results in the JavaScript Exploratorium.

## Using the Array( ) Constructor to Create Arrays

Since the release of Navigator 3 and Internet Explorer 3 (versions with the second release and later of the JavaScript engine), it has been possible to create arrays by using JavaScript's Array( ) constructor function. Let's examine how this is done.

# TASK 3B-2:
## Examining the Array() Constructor

1. **Click on the second example: 2. Using An Array Constructor.** The code is displayed in the bottom frame, and the results of running the code are displayed in the Results text box. The code is explained below:

```
1.  function makeGarden2 ( ) {
2.     var theResult = "";
3.     var myGarden = new Array();
4.     myGarden[0] = "parsnip";
5.     myGarden[1] = "asparagus";
6.     myGarden[2] = "jerusalem artichoke";
7.     myGarden[3] = "salsify";
8.     myGarden[4] = "golden bantam";
9.     for (i=0; i<myGarden.length; i++) {
10.       theResult+= i + ". " + myGarden[i] + "\n";
11.    }
12.    theResult += "(" + myGarden.length + " elements long.)";
13.    return theResult;
14. }
```

In line 3, the makeGarden2 function creates a new array object using the built-in Array( ) constructor. The new array, myGarden, is empty, having a length of 0. (Alternatively, you can pass the Array( ) constructor an array size, as in Array(5). This returns an array of the specified length, containing empty elements.) Lines 4 through 8 assign values to the array, creating new elements simply by referring to them.

As in the previous example, a loop retrieves elements from the array, separating them with line feed characters. The result is then returned to the statement that called the function.

## Using Strings to Index an Array

The previous examples use integer values to index, or refer to, a particular array element. You can also use strings to identify array elements, as in the following assignments:

```
garden["North Patch"] = "vegetables";
garden["South Patch"] = "herbs";
garden["West Border"] = "perennial flowers";
```

Elements identified in this manner behave more like properties than array elements. This approach is useful when you want to take a natural language approach to naming array elements. It can also make your code easier to understand. For example, herbs planted in the southern part of the garden is more obvious from a statement like `garden["South Patch"] = "herbs"` than a statement like `garden[1] = "herbs"`. On the other hand, when you need to process the entire contents of the array, looping through a numbered array is very convenient. You can't do this with a string-indexed array.

Lesson 3: Arrays   55

You can intermingle numbered elements and string-indexed elements in the same array, but unless you're using JavaScript 1.0, these different types of elements are kept separate and cannot be used interchangeably. In other words, you can't use a numbered index to refer to an element in one statement, and then use a string index to refer to it in another.

## Populating Arrays as You Create Them

You can populate arrays as you create them, as in the following example:

```
processors = new Array("AMD","Intel","Cyrix","Motorola");
```

This statement creates an array of four elements, indexed from 0 to 3. For example, the expression `processors[2]` returns the value `"Cyrix"`.

## Array Literals

Another way to populate arrays as you create them is to use *array literals*. In programming, a literal expression is meant to be taken literally; the expression is not the name of a variable or constant that holds a value, but the value itself. A literal expression creates a value on-the-fly. The following two statements use array literals:

```
doStuff( ["Shadrach","Meshach","Abednego"] );
processors = ["AMD","Intel","Cyrix","Motorola"];
```

In the first statement, the function call takes one argument: an array literal containing three elements. You can also assign array literals to a variable, as in the second statement. The second statement results in an array called `processors`, similar to the `processors` array we created in an earlier example, but this example doesn't use the `Array()` constructor at all.

**array literals:**
*A syntactic method of populating arrays as you create them.*

# TASK 3B-3:

## Examining an Array That is Populated Upon Creation

1.  **Click the third example: 3. Populating An Array As You Create It.** The code is displayed in the bottom frame, and the results of running the code are displayed in the Results text box.

    ```
    1. function makeGarden3 ( ) {
    2.   var theResult = "";
    3.   var myGarden = ["parsnip","asparagus","jerusalem ⇒
         artichoke", "salsify","golden bantam"];
    4.   for (i=0; i<myGarden.length; i++) {
    5.     theResult+= i + ". " + myGarden[i] + "\n";
    6.   }
    7.   theResult += "(" + myGarden.length + " elements long.)";
    8.   return theResult;
    9. }
    ```

    This example is similar to others that you have seen. In line 3, however, is a statement that assigns a variable to an array literal. After line 3 runs, myGarden refers to an array of five elements.

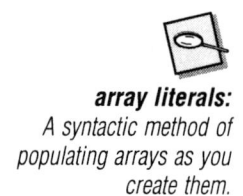

# Topic 3C

## Deleting Array Elements

At any time, you can change the value of an array element or add a new element to the array. But to delete an element along with its index, you must have JavaScript 1.2 or higher. This version of JavaScript introduced the `delete` operator, demonstrated below:

```
threeStooges = new Array("Curly","Moe","Shemp","Larry");
delete threeStooges[2];
```

The resulting array contains "Curly," "Moe," and "Larry."

Unfortunately, the `delete` operator does not change the length of the array. After the above statements run, the `length` of `threeStooges` is still 4. The expression `threeStooges[2]` evaluates as `undefined` because the value that was in the third element of the array no longer exists—even though the element itself does exist. To shorten the array, you must create a new array and copy only those elements from the original array that you want to keep. You could write a custom function to do this. The following task demonstrates such a function.

# TASK 3C-1:

## Adding a Method to Prune Elements From an Array

1. **Click the fourth example: 4. Pruning an array element.** The code is displayed in the bottom frame, and the results of running the code are displayed in the Results text box. The code is explained below:

```
1  // Prune array element
2  function pruneElement(theArray,theElement) {
3    tempArray = new Array();
4    for (i=0; i<theArray.length; i++) {
5      if (i != theElement)
6        tempArray[tempArray.length] = theArray[i];
7    }
8    return tempArray;
9  }
10
11 function pruneDemo ( ) {
12   newArray1 = new Array("Fibber","McGee","Molly");
13   var theResult = "    New: " + newArray1 +
14                   " (Length=" + newArray1.length +")";
15   delete newArray1[1];
```

```
16   theResult +=    "\nDeleted: " + newArray1 +
17                   " (Length=" + newArray1.length +")";
18
19   newArray2 = new Array("Fibber","McGee","Molly");
20   theResult += "\n\n   New: " + newArray2 +
21                   " (Length=" + newArray2.length +")";
22   newArray2 = pruneElement(newArray2,1);
23   theResult +=    "\n Pruned: " + newArray2 +
24                   " (Length=" + newArray2.length +")";
25   return theResult;
26 }
```

When the `pruneDemo()` function (line 11) runs, it creates a new array (line 12) containing three elements: `"Fibber"`, `"McGee"`, and `"Molly"`. Lines 13 and 14 put the contents and length of the array into a variable called `theResult` (which contains text that will be displayed in the Results text box after the function runs).

In line 15, the second element of the array (element 1) is deleted. Lines 16 and 17 put the new contents and length of the array into theResult.

Similar to lines 12 through 17, lines 19 through 24 create a new array, put its content and length into `theResult`, delete the second element, and then put the new contents and length of the array into `theResult`. However, line 22 uses the `pruneElement()` function to delete the second element of the new array.

The `pruneElement()` function begins in line 2. This function receives as arguments the array to be pruned and the element number that should be pruned. In line 3, a new, empty array is created to hold the "pruned" version of the array. The `for` loop in lines 4 through 7 copies each element of the original array into the new array, except for the element (line 5) that is supposed to be pruned. Line 8 returns the array—minus the specified element—to the calling statement.

As an alternative to using a function like `pruneElement()`, you could use the Array object's `pop()` method, which is supported in Navigator 4.0 (and later). However, `pop()` is not supported in Internet Explorer 5.0 and earlier versions.

## Destroying an Entire Array

To destroy an array, you can assign its `length` the value 0, or you can assign the value `null` to the array, as in the following statements:

```
1. myShortLivedArray = ["Only","the","good","die","young"];
2. whatsaMeaningOfLife = ["To","love","and","be","loved"];
3. myShortLivedArray.length = 0;
4. whatsaMeaningOfLife = null;
```

After these statements run, `myShortLivedArray` still contains an array, but it has a length of 0 and has no elements. However, `whatsaMeaningOfLife` will not contain an array. In fact, it will refer to no object at all. The method you use to destroy the array depends on what you want to do with it later. If you are going to add elements to the array again, set its length to 0 to clear out its elements. If you want to totally destroy the array, set it to `null`. Of course, another option is to just ignore the array when you are done with it. The browser will automatically destroy the array when the user moves to another page.

# Topic 3D

## Multi-dimensional Arrays

JavaScript arrays are one-dimensional—for example, they have width, but no height.

Certain types of information lend themselves to being stored in matrices. Calculation worksheets, charts and graphs, tests and quizzes, and even games such as Battleship, checkers, chess, and Pac-Man are naturally stored in two-dimensional arrays. A third dimension might be added to represent space, and a fourth dimension might be added to represent time.

If you have programmed in other languages that are capable of multi-dimensional arrays (that is, matrices), this lack of dimension may seem like an unfortunate limitation of JavaScript arrays. Fortunately, there are several ways around this limitation.

## Parallel Arrays

A simple approach to adding dimension to JavaScript arrays is to simply add more of them. *Parallel arrays* are sets of arrays that are the same length, with related data stored at the same index in each array. Let's look at an example of parallel arrays to see how they work together.

# TASK 3D-1:
## Examining Parallel Arrays

*parallel arrays:*
*Sets of arrays that are the same length, with related data stored at the same index in each array.*

1. In the Arrays lab, **click on 5. Parallel Arrays.** In the Results text box, the following is displayed:

   ```
   PARALLEL ARRAY RESULTS:

   black snakeroot is called cimicifuga racemosa
   foxglove is called digitalis purpurea
   yarrow is called achillea
   ```

   Each of these statements contains two names of a particular herb. First is the English name (yarrow) followed by the Latin name (achillea). This was produced from a lookup table that consists of two parallel arrays.

Lesson 3: Arrays 59

2. **Examine the code for the parallel arrays.**

```
function parArray() {
  var theResult = "";
  herb =  ["black snakeroot","foxglove","yarrow"]
  latin = ["cimicifuga racemosa","digitalis ⇒
purpurea","achillea"]
  for (i=0; i < herb.length; i++) {
    theResult += herb[i] + " is called " + latin[i] + "\n"
  }
  return theResult;
}
```

The parallel arrays are herb and latin. It is assumed that corresponding elements are stored in the same position in each array. With each pass through the loop, the element i of the herb array is followed by the element i of the latin array.

## Nested Arrays

Sometimes, it's useful to be able to refer to values using a coordinate system, such as the one shown in Figure 3-1.

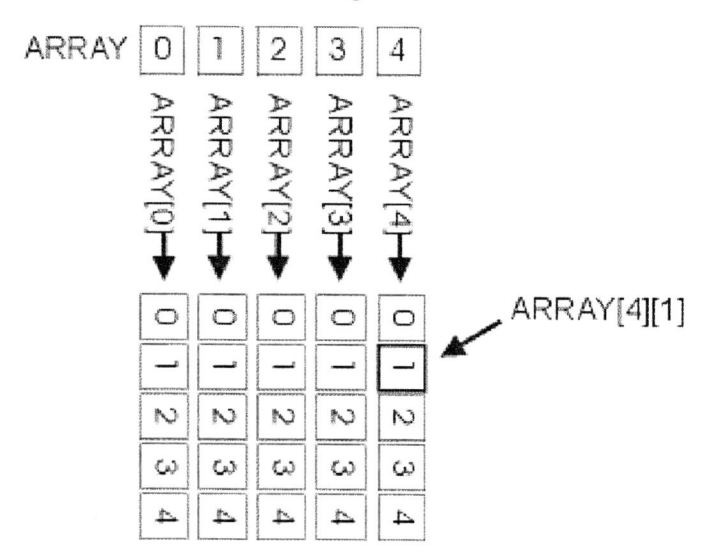

**Figure 3-1:** *Nested arrays*

For example, the element in the 5th column, 2nd row would be element (4,1). If your base index is 1 (rather than 0), the coordinates for the element in the 5th column, 2nd row would be (5,2). If you need to have a third dimension, you could add another coordinate, as in (5,2,4). This is the element in the 5th column, 2nd row, 4th element deep.

# TASK 3D-2:

## Examining Nested Arrays

1. In the Arrays lab, **click on 6. Nested Arrays (Tic-Tac-Toe).** You are prompted to enter a row, from 1 to 3.

2. **Type a number (1, 2, or 3) and click on OK.** You are prompted to enter a column, from 1 to 3.

3. **Enter a column number and click on OK.** An "X" appears in a 3-by-3 tic-tac-toe grid in the Results box, at the location you specified.

4. **Review the following code:**

```
1  function twoCol() {
2    tictactoe = new Array(3);
3    tictactoe[0] = new Array(3);
4    tictactoe[1] = new Array(3);
5    tictactoe[2] = new Array(3);
6
7    // Fill the board with spaces
8    for (var y=0; y <= 2; y++) {
9      for (var x=0; x <= 2; x++) {
10       self.window.status = "Loc " + x + ", " + y;
11       tictactoe[x][y] = " ";
12     }
13   }
14
15   theRow = prompt("Select a row (1-3)","2");
16   theCol = prompt("Select a column (1-3)", "2");
17   if (((theRow>=1)&&(theRow<=3))&&((theCol>=1)&& ⇒
(theCol<=3))) {
18     // Place an X in the upper right
19     tictactoe[theCol-1][theRow-1] = "X";
20
21     // Return the results
22     var theResult = "+-+-+-+\n";   // Begin grid
23     for (y=0; y<=2; y++) {
24       for (x=0; x<=2; x++) {
25         theResult += "|" + tictactoe[x][y];
26       }
27       theResult += "|\n+-+-+-+\n";
28     }
29   }
30   return theResult;
31 }
```

Line 2 creates a new array that contains three elements. Lines 3 through 5 assign to each element of the new array another new array of three elements, creating a 3-by-3 matrix.

Lines 8 through 13 put a space into each element of the matrix. Notice the statement that makes the assignment in line 11. This statement refers to two arrays: the first part of the expression, tictactoe[x], returns element x of the tictactoe array (this actually refers to another array); the [y] specifies that we want to assign a value to element y of that array.

Lines 22 through 30 contain statements that read each element of the array, and format them to appear in a grid. Reading from nested arrays is very similar to the process for writing.

## Nesting Arrays Within an Object

Of course, this [x][y] notation is bit odd. People are used to seeing coordinates written in the form (x,y). By managing nested arrays within a custom object, you can make a matrix that uses notation that is more familiar. Let's look at an example.

## TASK 3D-3:

### Examining and Extending a Matrix Object

1. In the Arrays lab, **click 7. Matrix Object Demo.** This demo illustrates how a matrix custom object might be implemented. The example matrix used in the demo is a rack of video tapes, such as you might find in a video rental store.

```
function matrix(x,y) {
  this.mat = new Array(x);
  for (i=0; i<(x-1); i++) {
    this.mat[i] = new Array(y);
  }
  this.get = matrix_get;
  this.put = matrix_put;
}

function matrix_get(x,y) {
  return this.mat[x][y];
}

function matrix_put(x,y,value) {
  this.mat[x][y] = value;
}

function matDemo() {
  // Create matrix
  movieRack = new matrix(300,12);
  // Store item in matrix
  movieRack.put(1,4,"Feivel Goes West");
  // Read item from matrix
  return movieRack.get(1,4);
}
```

This example simply hides the nested arrays approach you saw in the previous task within an object. The three lines in the matDemo function demonstrate how to create, write to, and read from a matrix by using this object. In this simple example, a shelf system is created to hold 300 racks, 12 shelves high. The movie "Feivel Goes West" is stored in rack 1, shelf 4; then it is read back to the Results text box.

You could implement matrices with even more dimensions using similar (albeit more complicated) techniques.

# Apply Your Knowledge 3-1

**Suggested Time:** *30 minutes*

## Extending the Matrix Object

In this activity, you will give the Matrix custom object the following new properties and methods:

- `count`—returns `width` times `height`. Given the width and height examples above (50 and 25), `count` would return `1250`.
- `width`—accepts no arguments and returns the number of columns (x values) in the matrix. For example, if x elements in the matrix range from `0` to `49`, then `width` would return `50`.
- `height`—accepts no arguments and returns the number of rows (y values) in the matrix. For example, if y elements in the matrix range from `0` to `24`, then height would return `25`.
- `setDimensions`—accepts x and y values, and changes the size of the matrix according to the values passed. Although the matrix object uses zero-based indices, the value of x and y passed to `setDimensions` refer to the count of elements in each dimension. Therefore, `aMatrix.setDimensions(100,50)` would resize the matrix to have column elements from 0 to 99, and row elements from 0 to 49.

The `width`, `height`, and `count` items could be implemented as properties or methods, but `setDimensions` must be implemented as a method.

1. In the JavaScript Adv Prog folder, open the folder Lab - Arrays. This folder contains files that you will modify in this lab.

2. Open the folder Solution. This folder contains finished versions of the files that you will modify in this lab.

3. In your Web browser, open Matrix.htm. A text box labeled "Matrix Info" informs you that a 300-by-300 matrix (90,000 cells total) has been created. Other buttons and text boxes enable you to store or retrieve a value from any cell of this matrix, and resize the matrix to new dimensions.

4. In the X Location text box, enter *50*, and in the Y Location text box, enter *50*.

5. In the Value text box, enter your name.

6. Click the Store button to store your name in the cell (50,50).

7. Delete your name from the Value text box and click on Retrieve. Your name reappears. It was retrieved from the specified cell (50,50).

8. In the Width text box, enter *100*, and in the Height text box, enter *300*.

9. Click on Resize To These Dimensions. The Matrix Info text box is updated to display the new dimensions.

10. Clear your name from the Value text box, and click on Retrieve. Your name is restored. Even though you increased the size of the matrix, its original contents have been kept intact.

11. Resize the matrix to a width of 10 and a height of 10. (Be sure to click on "Resize to these dimensions" after you enter the new width and height.)

12. Click on Retrieve. The value of cell (50,50) is undefined because the matrix is now only 10 cells wide by 10 cells tall. You deleted the part of the matrix that held your name.

13. Exit the browser application and return to the folder Lab - Arrays (in the JavaScript Adv Prog folder).

14. Open Matrix.htm in your Web browser. (Make sure you don't open the version that is in the Solution folder.)

15. Attempt to resize the matrix. An error occurs because this feature is not yet functional in this version of the document. You must create the `setDimensions` method, which is used to resize the matrix. A section of the code in this document is shown below. Notice the expressions in bold, which refer to the method and properties that you will implement in this activity.

```
<HTML>
<HEAD>
<TITLE>Matrix Object</TITLE>
<SCRIPT language="JavaScript"
                src="..\explore\bugs\debug.js">
</SCRIPT>

<SCRIPT language="JavaScript" src="matrix.js"></SCRIPT>

<SCRIPT language="JavaScript">

var demoMatrix = new matrix(300,300);

function updateInfo() {
  var theInfo = "MATRIX INFORMATION\n";
  theInfo += "Height: " + demoMatrix.height + "\n";
  theInfo += "Width: " + demoMatrix.width + "\n";
  theInfo += "Number of cells: " + ⇒
  demoMatrix.count + "\n";
  document.theForm.txtInfo.value = theInfo;
}

function resize() {
  var x = parseInt(document.theForm.txtWidth.value);
  var y = parseInt(document.theForm.txtHeight.value);
  if (!isNaN(x) && !isNaN(y)) {
     demoMatrix.setDimensions(x,y);
  }
  updateInfo();
}

function store() {
  demoMatrix.put(parseInt(document.theForm.txtX.value),
             parseInt(document.theForm.txtY.value),
             document.theForm.txtValue.value);
}

function retrieve() {
 document.theForm.txtValue.value =
    demoMatrix.get(parseInt(document.theForm.txtX.value),
```

```
        parseInt(document.theForm.txtY.value));
}
</SCRIPT>
</HEAD>

<BODY bgcolor=silver onload="updateInfo()">
<FORM name=theForm>
<P align=center><STRONG><FONT face=Arial>
Matrix Info:<BR></FONT></STRONG>
<TEXTAREA cols=60
          name=txtInfo
          rows=5>
          </TEXTAREA>
</P>
<TABLE width=500 border=1 align=center>
  <TR align=middle>
    <TD>
    <INPUT type=button
        name=btnResize
        value="Resize to these dimensions:"
        onClick="resize()"> Width:
    <INPUT name=txtWidth size=5> Height:
    <INPUT name=txtHeight size=5>
    </TD>
  </TR>
</TABLE>

<TABLE width=500 border=1 align=center>
  <TR>
    <TD width=15% align=right rowspan=2>
    <INPUT type=button
        name=btnStore
        value=Store
        onClick= store()"><BR>
    <INPUT type=button
        name=btnRetrieve
        value =Retrieve
        onClick="retrieve()">
    </TD>
    <TD width=26%>
    <DIV align=center>X Location:
      <INPUT name=txtX size=5>
    </DIV>
    </TD>
    <TD width=59% rowspan=2>
      <DIV align=center>Value:
      <INPUT name=txtValue size=30>
    </DIV>
    </TD>
  </TR>
  <TR>
```

```
            <TD width=26%>
            <DIV align=center>Y Location:
              <INPUT name=txtY size=5>
            </DIV>
            </TD>
          </TR>
        </TABLE>
      </FORM>

    </BODY>
</HTML>
```

16. Dismiss the error message and exit the browser application.

17. Open Matrix.js in your text editor. In this file are all of the declarations for the Matrix object. All of the modifications that you make in this activity will be within this file.

    ```
    function matrix(x,y) {
      this.mat = new Array(x);
      for (i=0; i<(x-1); i++) {
        this.mat[i] = new Array(y);
      }
      this.get = matrix_get;
      this.put = matrix_put;
    }
    function matrix_get(x,y) {
      if (this.mat.length >x) {
        if (this.mat[x].length > y) {
          return this.mat[x][y];
        }
      }
    }

    function matrix_put(x,y,value) {
      if (this.mat.length > x) {
        if (this.mat[x].length > y) {
          this.mat[x][y] = value;
        }
      }
    }
    ```

18. Add the setDimensions method and the width, height, and count properties to the Matrix object, as described at the beginning of this activity.

19. To test your work, open the Matrix.htm file in your Web browser. (Be sure you don't open the version of Matrix.htm that is in the Solutions folder, but rather the one that is in Lab - Arrays.) Perform steps 4 through 12 of this activity, verifying that the document that you modified behaves the same way that the solution file behaved.

## Summary

In this lesson, you examined ways in which arrays can be used. You learned how arrays are created and populated with data. You also learned how to delete array elements and how to destroy an entire array. Finally, you created custom objects to simplify the creation and management of arrays with single and multiple dimensions.

# Lesson Review

**3A** Explain why it is beneficial to place data within array structures.

**3B** Write one or more statements that create an array named `myJobs`, and populate it with the following entries:
- Butcher
- Baker
- Web Developer

**3C** Write a statement that deletes the data value held in the third element in the array `myFavoriteThings` without deleting the element itself.

Write a statement that deletes all elements (so that its length is zero) from the array `myFavoriteThings`, without destroying the array.

**3D** Given the following statements, what statement would you write to put the value "50" into the third column, first row of the matrix?

```
tictactoe = new Array(3);
tictactoe[0] = new Array(3);
tictactoe[1] = new Array(3);
tictactoe[2] = new Array(3);
```

# Displaying and Manipulating Data Tables

## LESSON 4

## Overview

In this lesson, you will load data into code that manipulates data tables, both in hard-coded and in delimited file form; then, you will construct functionality that selects, sorts, and searches data tables for display on a Web page.

## Objectives

To build functionality that can manipulate data tables, you will:

**4A** **Load data into an application that displays and manipulates data tables.**

After exploring the functionality of the select, sort, and search controls for a data table application, you will craft the code necessary to successfully load data into the application—either by explicit assignment of data items, or by using a data-loading function to process data in delimited files.

**4B** **Create code that selects fields from a data table for display.**

Given a frameset document and populated Select object as a data control, you will craft the necessary code for selecting data, by field, from a two-dimensional array for output in a dynamically-created HTML table structure.

**4C** **Create code that searches on a single field from a data table for display.**

Given a frameset document and populated Select object as a data control, you will craft the necessary code for searching data by field from a two-dimensional array for output in a dynamically-created HTML table structure.

**4D** **Create code that sorts on a single field from a data table for display.**

Given a frameset document and populated Select object as a data control, you will craft the necessary code for sorting data by field from a two-dimensional array for output in a dynamically-created HTML table structure.

**Data Files**
DTProject.html
DTLeft.html
DTRight.html
zodiac.js
birthstones.js
lighthouses.js
DTLeft2.html
wines.js
displarr.html
selectfields.html
vino.js
searchfields.html
sortfields.html
blank.html

**Lesson Time**
1 hour, 15 minutes

# Topic 4A

## Loading Data

Let it be said at the outset: using JavaScript to provide functionality for manipulating data tables isn't drawing on one of the language's strengths, especially now that many technologies have been specifically designed to power dynamic Web sites with server-side databases on the back end. However, for modest projects that involve amounts of data that won't adversely affect the download time of your pages, you can provide simple controls to manipulate data tables.

Data table manipulation is based on three main operations:

- *Selecting data*—winnowing down subsets of information from a larger set; for example, drawing a list of the last names and political parties of the the U.S. presidents from a larger list that also includes each president's home state and the dates for birth, death, and term served.

- *Sorting data*—rearranging displayed records in an ascending or descending alpha-numeric order; for example, a list of the U.S. presidents by home state, from Alabama to Wyoming.

- *Searching data*—displaying information based on an entered criterion; for example, a list of the U.S. presidents whose names begin with the letter *R*.

In terms of architecture, the data table manipulation functionality you will work with in this lesson consists of the following parts:

- A *frameset document* that loads frames for data controls and data output.

- A *data control document* that loads, manipulates, and displays data.

- A blank *data output document* used as a placeholder for displaying data from the data control document.

- A *data document* that holds the data pulled into the data control document by way of a `<SCRIPT>` include. Usually, data is coded into a two-dimensional array in the data document in one of two ways:

    — *Hard-coded:* Each data item is explicitly defined by a JavaScript assignment statement that deposits the item into an array element.

    — *Processed:* Data items stored as records in a delimited format are loaded into the array by a series of function calls.

# TASK 4A-1:
## Exploring a Data Table Manipulation Application

1. In your browser, **open the file DTProject.html.**

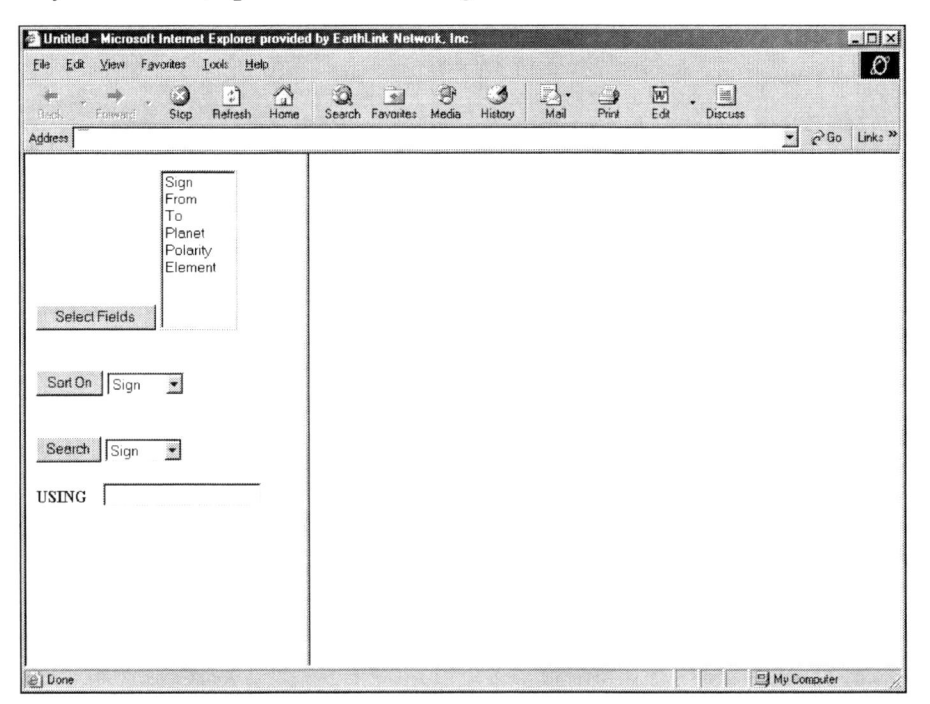

   [Screenshot of browser window showing the DTProject.html application with a left frame containing Select Fields list (Sign, From, To, Planet, Polarity, Element), Sort On dropdown, Search dropdown, and USING field.]

   It displays a data table manipulation application. The application is deployed as a frameset: the left frame (DTLeft.html) contains the data controls; the right frame (DTRight.html) is the data table viewing area.

2. In the left frame, **explore the functionality of the data controls.** They enable you to select fields for viewing, to sort the table on a single field, and to perform partial-word searches on a single field. Currently, they operate on data about the zodiac signs.

3. In your editor, **open the files DTLeft.html and DTRight.html** to see if you can find the data displayed in the right frame.

   **Were you successful?**

4. In your editor, **open the file zodiac.js.** It contains the data table.

   **How is the data from zodiac.js included in the DTProject.html application?**

*To refresh the application, you must place your insertion point in the URL Locator and press [Enter].*

Lesson 4: Displaying and Manipulating Data Tables 71

> Is the data in zodiac.js hard-coded into the array, or is it processed from a delimited file? Why?

5. In your editor, in the file DTLeft.html, **locate the following code:**

   `<SCRIPT LANGUAGE="JavaScript" SRC="zodiac.js"></SCRIPT>`

6. **Modify the code to the following:**

   `<SCRIPT LANGUAGE="JavaScript" SRC="birthstones.js"></SCRIPT>`

   The file birthstones.js contains a data table about birthstones.

7. **Save your changes.**

8. In your browser, **reload DTProject.html.** This time, a new list of field names appears in the Select objects; when used, they cause information from the new data table to be displayed.

9. **View the source code for the file birthstones.js.** You will see that the data has been hard-coded into the two-dimensional array via assignment statements for each data point.

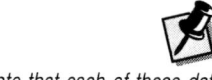

*Note that each of these data tables contains the same number of records.*

## Data Tables as Array Objects

In the parlance of the database world, data housed in a data table is organized in two ways: *by record*, in which different kinds of information are related into a single grouping; and *by field*, in which a single kind of information is related across records. For example, a record's-worth of data in a telephone book consists of the last name, first name, address, and telephone number for an individual. Likewise, a field's-worth of information is a list of all the telephone numbers in the phone book.

Usually, records are viewed in the rows of a data table, and fields, by column.

Translating the dual nature of a table's records and fields into JavaScript is straight-forward: by using a two-dimensional array, you can set the first dimension as the "record" of the table, and the second dimension as the "fields."

## Hard-coding Array Objects

To hard-code a data table as a two-dimensional array, consider the first numeric coordinate of the array syntax as the record number, and the second coordinate as the field number. For example, say you had the following telephone directory information:

| Last Name: | First Name: | Street: | Number: |
|---|---|---|---|
| Adams | Dan | 132 Main St. | 555-1234 |
| Burgess | Candi | 234 South Ave. | 555-2435 |
| Boatwright | Darryl | 345 Norton Blvd. | 555-4567 |

Hard-coding these data items into a two-dimensional array would appear thus:

```
phoneArr[0][0] = "Last Name"
phoneArr[0][1] = "First Name"
phoneArr[0][2] = "Street"
phoneArr[0][3] = "Number"

phoneArr[1][0] = "Adams"
phoneArr[1][1] = "Dan"
phoneArr[1][2] = "132 Main Street"
phoneArr[1][3] = "555-1234"

phoneArr[2][0] = "Burgess"
phoneArr[2][1] = "Candi"
phoneArr[2][2] = "234 South Avenue"
phoneArr[2][3] = "555-2435"

phoneArr[3][0] = "Boatwright"
phoneArr[3][1] = "Darryl"
phoneArr[3][2] = "345 Norton Blvd."
phoneArr[3][3] = "555-4567"
```

Note that the table headers are also coded into the array as the $0^{th}$ record, or *header record*.

Not only must you create a two-dimensional array for the hard-coded data itself, but also for any other Array objects that might be needed for temporarily holding, sorting, and displaying the data in the course of processing. (This will be apparent as you progress through the lesson). The important thing to remember is that if you use several Array objects to manipulate a data table, try to make their structure identical, in terms of what data items go where, to retain consistency.

## Pointer Arrays

A useful tool for manipulating the output of a data table from a two-dimensional array is the pointer array. *Pointer arrays* do not contain data from the data table, but rather, the record numbers that can be used to generate different record orderings for output. Consider the following pointer array:

```
var pointArr = new Array(0,1,3,2);
```

If its elements were evaluated as record numbers for generating a table of last names from `phoneArr` above (that is, directed your code to display record 0, record 1, record 3, and *then* record 2), the table would be alphabetized.

Note that pointer arrays don't change the location of data in the array, but rather, keep track of the order in which the records should be processed based on their *existing* location.

**header record:**
Usually the first record of a data table housed in a two-dimensional array table, used to store the name of the array's fields.

**pointer array:**
An array used to house record numbers so that the rows of a data table can be reordered.

# TASK 4A-2:

## Instantiating a Data Table Array From Hard-coded Data

1. In your editor, **open the file lighthouses.js.** The file contains a a two-dimensional array named `recArr`. The array holds a data table about lighthouses that has been hard-coded in data assignment statements.

2. Examine the assignment statements, and then answer the following questions:

   **How many records are in the data table?**

   **How many fields are in each record?**

   **What is the purpose of the first record?**

3. At the top of the document, **instantiate three Array objects** under the following names:
   - `tempArr`
   - `recArr`
   - `rSet`

   These three arrays manage the data table at various points. The `recArr` array holds the data in its original form; `tempArr` temporarily holds a data subset; and `rSet` receives from `tempArr` and displays the data subset. In terms of size, these three arrays must be identical, because the total amount of information they hold is the same.

4. Under your previous work, **enter the following code:**

   ```
   for(recnum = 0; recnum < 45; recnum++)
      {
      tempArr[recnum] = new Array();
      recArr[recnum] = new Array();
      rSet[recnum] = new Array();
      }
   ```

   **What does this code block do?**

74  *JavaScript: Advanced Programming (Second Edition)*

5. Under your previous work, **instantiate an Array object named `pointArr`.** It is a pointer array that, instead of holding the data, holds a set of record numbers whose ordering and reordering enables the application to display the data table under different criteria.

6. Within the assignment statement you just coded for the `pointArr` array, **enter the numbers zero to 44** such that the `pointArr` holds each number as an individual element, for a total of 45 elements.

   `pointArr = new Array(0,1,2,3,4...etc...44);`

7. **Save your work.** In your editor, in the file DTLeft2.html, under the comment, **enter a `<SCRIPT>` include** to pull in the data table stored in the lighthouses.js file. Then, in the file DTProject.html, **modify the `SRC` attribute of the first frame** so that DTLeft2.html is displayed, not DTLeft.html.

8. **Save and test your work.** After you reload DTProject.html, the lighthouses data table should be displayed when you operate the data controls in your browser.

*If for some reason your data was entered in an order that you didn't want to view by default, you could "reorder" the records with the list of arguments in `pointArr`.*

*Don't forget to add the closing `</SCRIPT>` tag.*

## Creating Data Table Array Objects From Delimited Files

Although hard-coding data tables into an Array object enables you to "see it all" in terms of loading data items into array elements, it is very typing-intensive. And what's more, data existing in other formats must often be completely re-typed to be entered correctly in your JavaScript code.

Fortunately, there is another way—the delimited files approach.

You might know that *delimited files* present table data as a series of items separated by a delimiter, such as a comma. Like a table, each line (row) of a delimited file represents a data record, and the individual items separated by commas, the record's fields. Thus, the telephone book entries you saw earlier could be represented in a delimited file with the following format:

```
"Last Name","First Name","Street","Number"
"Adams","Dan","132 Main St.","555-1234"
"Burgess","Candi","234 South Ave.","555-2435"
"Boatwright","Darryl","345 Norton Blvd.","555-4567"
```

Since each record in a delimited file has a syntax identical to an arguments list for a function, it's possible to wrap each record in a function call that can then load the record into an Array object:

```
loadMe("Last Name","First Name","Street","Number")
loadMe("Adams","Dan","132 Main St.","555-1234")
loadMe("Burgess","Candi","234 South Ave.","555-2435")
loadMe("Boatwright","Darryl","345 Norton Blvd.","555-4567")
```

Once passed to the hypothetical `loadMe()` function, these data-items-now-arguments can be assigned into an Array object's elements by using a combination of nested loops and the Function object's built-in `arguments` array.

**delimited file:**
*A data table whose records are presented in rows having fields separated by a symbol, such as a comma.*

Lesson 4: Displaying and Manipulating Data Tables  75

# TASK 4A-3:

## Creating a Data Table Array From Delimited Files

1. In your editor, **open the file wines.js.** For the most part, it is a delimited data file that contains a record's-worth of data on each line of the document. Note that each data record contains the same number of data items; since some are empty, two double-quotes mark the position of empty data points.

2. At the top of the file, **locate the following code:**

   ```
   var tempArr = new Array();
   var rSet = new Array();
   var recArr = new Array();

   var pointArr = new Array(0,1,2,3,.etc. .27);
   ```

   This code instantiates the same three data table Array objects as before, along with the pointer array. Since there are 28 lines of delimited data, the pointer array is hard-coded to contain 28 arguments (from zero to 27).

3. For each record, **encase the data items within a call to a function named buildDT():**

   ```
   buildDT(data items for first record...);
   buildDT(data items for second record...);
   buildDT(data items for third record...);
   buildDT(data items for fourth record...);
   etc....
   ```

   These function calls transform the data records into lists of arguments.

4. In between the array instantiation statements and the function calls, **enter the following code:**

   ```
   recnum = 0;

   function buildDT()
     {
     tempArr[recnum] = new Array();
     recArr[recnum] = new Array();
     rSet[recnum] = new Array();

     for(i = 0; i < arguments.length; i++)
        {
        recArr[recnum][i] = arguments[i];
        }
     recnum += 1;
     }
   ```

   Here's what `buildDT()` does:
   - The variable `recnum` is a global variable that starts at zero and counts the number of times the `buildDT()` function gets called. Even though it is used and modified within the function, it is not destroyed when the function completes its task. Ultimately, it counts the total number of records in the data table.

- Each time `buildDT()` is called, `recnum` adds a new element to each of the three arrays, which is then assigned a newly instantiated Array object; this forms the arrays' second dimension.
- The `for` loop uses the function's built-in `arguments` array to assign the data values for the record into the elements housed in `recArr` array's second dimension. The `arguments` array's `length` property defines how many times the loop iterates; it is equal to the number of data items that exist in the record being processed.
- The `recnum` variable is incremented at the end of the function; at that point, it is equal to the length of the arrays' first dimension (the number of records existing in the arrays).

5. **Save your work.**

6. In your editor, **open the file DTLeft2.html.** In the `<SCRIPT>` include tag for the data table, **modify the SRC attribute** to link wines.js to DTLeft2.html.

7. In your browser, **load DTProject.html** to test your work. The new data table should be displayed when you manipulate the data controls.

# Topic 4B

## Selecting Data for Display

The process for selecting fields from a data table for display as an HTML table involves:

1. Determining what fields are selected.
2. Cycling through the entire data table to access the selected data.
3. Assembling an HTML table from the selected data.

The easiest way to determine what fields the user wants displayed is to use a select-multiple list whose options correspond to the ordering of the fields in the two-dimensional array housing the data table. That way, the index numbering between the options in the Select object and the field numbers in the two-dimensional array are identical.

To cycle throught all the data values housed in a two-dimensional array, you must use a nested loop structure:

```
for(recno = 0; recno < array.length; recno++)
   {
   for(fldno = 0; fldno < array[recno].length; fldno++)
      {
      document.write(array[recno][fldno]);
      }
   document.write("<BR>");
   }
```

*Lesson 4: Displaying and Manipulating Data Tables* **77**

In the example above, the outer loop's counter, `recno`, moves through the array, record-by-record. Within each of the outer loop's iterations, the inner loop's counter, `fldno`, moves through the fields of the record, field-by-field. Note that the values in the `for` loops measure the number of records and the number of fields in the currently evaluated record, respectively, to control the cut-off point for the loops.

Within the inner loop is a `document.write()` statement that outputs the currently accessed data value from the array to the document. Note that a <BR> tag is placed into the output stream directly after the inner loop has finished and before the outer loop moves on to the next record.

By the completion of the outer loop, all the data values will have been accessed and output to the document with each record's worth of data on its own line (but not in HTML table format). Inserting the necessary coding to place the data into an HTML table format consists of adding a few strategically-placed lines of code:

```
document.write("<TABLE>");
for(recno = 0; recno < array.length; recno++)
    {
    document.write("<TR>");
    for(fldno = 0; fldno < array[recno].length; fldno++)
        {
        document.write("<TD>");
        document.write(array[recno][fldno]);
        document.write("</TD>");
        }
    document.write("</TR>");
    }
document.write("</TABLE>");
```

Except for the opening and closing <TABLE> tags, the tag output statements begin and end the code held within the loop.

At this point, a mechanism can be inserted into the structure that allows for fields to be included or not included according to the user's interaction. On its simplest terms, this mechanism can use a Select object whose list of options presents the data table's field names in the same order as the list of fields in the array. That way, the index for the Select object's `options[]` array has the same meaning as the index for the array's fields. Inserting the mechanism into the code example would appear thus:

```
document.write("<TABLE>");
for(recno = 0; recno < array.length; recno++)
    {
    document.write("<TR>");
    for(fldno = 0; fldno < array[recno].length; fldno++)
        {
        if(selobj.options[fldno].selected)
            {
            document.write("<TD>");
            document.write(array[recno][fldno]);
            document.write("</TD>");
            }
        }
    document.write("</TR>");
    }
document.write("</TABLE>");
```

Note that the central aspect of the select feature is the use of the option's `selected` property. It indicates whether the user selected the option in the list: if `true`, the corresponding data item from the array is included in the output; if `false`, the data item is skipped.

Although this example uses the `document.write()` method to assemble the data within an HTML table structure, you can also use other techniques—among them, concatenating the table's rows into an output variable for later use in your code.

# TASK 4B-1:
## Coding the Select Functionality

1. In your browser, **open the file displarr.html.** It is a pared-down version of the data table application you worked with in the last topic. In its left frame, a multiple-select list containing the field names of a data table is visible, along with a non-functional button. In its right frame is a blank display area for the fields users will select from the list for viewing.

2. In your editor, **open selectfields.html.** This is the file that loads into the left frame of displarr.html. Take a minute to **locate the following items** in selectfields.html:

    - A Form object named `MyForm`.
    - A Select object named `SelObj`, with several options listing the field names of a data table about lighthouses.
    - A Button object named `selbut`.
    - A `<SCRIPT>` include tag pair that pulls in the lighthouses.js data table as a two-dimensional array named `recArr`.

3. In the `<HEAD>` section of the document, within the blank `<SCRIPT>` tags, **enter the following code:**

```
function selflds(selobj)
  {
  var output = "";
  for(i = 0; i < recArr.length; i++)
    {
    output += "<TR>";
    for(j = 0; j < recArr[i].length; j++)
      {
      if(selobj.options[j].selected)
        {
        output += "<TD>" + recArr[i][j] + "</TD>";
        }
      }
    output += "</TR>";
    }
  top.frames[1].document.open();
  top.frames[1].document.write("<TABLE>");
  top.frames[1].document.write(output);
  top.frames[1].document.write("</TABLE>");
  top.frames[1].document.close();
  }
```

Lesson 4: Displaying and Manipulating Data Tables  79

Here's how the function works:

- After receiving a Select object as a passed parameter, the function declares a blank string in the variable `output`. This variable eventually will have concatenated into it a dynamically-created set of table rows and cells—in other words, the body of the HTML table structure that will be displayed in the right frame.
- The outer `i` loop cycles through the records of the two-dimensional array, record-by-record. Note that the beginning of each record iteration adds an opening `<TR>` tag to begin the new row of the table.
- Within the `i` loop, the `j` loop cycles through the fields of each record, field-by-field.
- The `if` statement within the `j` loop uses the `selected` property of each option of the Select object as a way to "pick out" the fields within each record selected by the user. Since the index numbering between the Select object and the data table is identical, each field in a record corresponds to an option in the Select object. Thus, if an option is selected, its corresponding field value from the data table is concatenated into the `output` variable with surrounding `<TD>` tags.
- Once the `j` loop cycles through a record's fields, the closing `</TR>` tag is concatenated to the `output` variable before the `i` loop iterates to the next record. By the end of the two loops, the `output` variable contains a series of HTML table rows, with each row containing the fields selected by the user.
- Here's what the series of output statements do:
  - The `document.open()` statement opens a new Document object in the right frame.
  - The `document.write("<TABLE>")` statement places the opening tag to an HTML table into the new Document object.
  - The `document.write(output)` statement places the table's body (its rows) after the `<TABLE>` tag.
  - The `document.write("</TABLE>")` statement closes the HTML table structure.
  - The `document.close()` statement closes the output stream to the new Document object.

4. Let's hook up this function. In the Form object, in the `<INPUT>` tag for the button, **add the following code:**

```
<INPUT
 TYPE="button"
 NAME="selbut"
 VALUE="Select Fields for Display"
 onClick="selflds(document.MyForm.SelObj);">
```

Note that the parameter passed in the function call is the named Select object from the form. Your selecting feature is now functional.

5. **Save and test your work.** You should be able to select various combinations of fields from the select-multiple list in the left frame, and then click the button to have them displayed in table format in the right frame.

# Topic 4C

## Searching Data for Display

Searching fields from a data table for display as an HTML table involves the following process:

1. Obtaining the following information from the user:
   - a text-based search criterion; and
   - a selected field to apply the criterion to.
2. Creating a Regular Expression (RegExp) object based on the criterion.
3. Creating a pointer array to hold the record numbers of records for output.
4. Using the RegExp object to test the data values for the field across the records of data in the table:
   - If the data value passes the test, its record number is recorded into the pointer array.
   - If the data value does not pass the test, its record number is not recorded.
5. Using the values in the pointer array to dynamically build a table of records housing data values that meet the criterion.

## Using the RegExp Object

Most often, you use a text box in a Form object to obtain text information for use as a search criterion. In other words, you can access the text entered by users in it to define a RegExp object that tests the data:

```
<FORM NAME="frmName">
<INPUT TYPE="text" NAME="txtName">
</FORM>
```

Using the text box defined in the example above, you can use the following syntax to create a RegExp Object from the text box's contents:

```
// Form object containing the text box...

<FORM NAME="frmName">
<INPUT TYPE="text" NAME="txtName">
</FORM>

// Statement creating the RegExp object...

var MyRegExp = new RegExp(document.frmName.txtName.value);
```

Once established with the criterion, you can use the RegExp object's `test()` method to test a field:

```
MyRegExp.test(arrayName[recno][fldno])
```

Note that `recno` and `fldno` can be numbers, variable names that hold numbers (such as a loop counter), or object property values (such as the Select object's `selectedIndex` property).

## Searching the Array

Believe it or not, you don't have to use a nested loop to search the data table when you build a single-term, partial-word search function. This is because the field the user selects in the Select object to search on defines the field number to be searched. All that's left is to cycle through the records looking for matches with the RegExp object:

```
function search(selobj)
  {
  code defining myRegExp...

  var pointerArray = new Array();
  pointerArray[0] = 0;

  counter = 1;
  for(m = 1; m < array.length; m++)
    {
    if(myRegExp.test(array[m][selobj.selectedIndex]))
      {
      pointArr[counter] = m;
      counter++
      }
    }
```

In the example above, the function is passed the Select object holding the field specified by the user to search on; then, the m loop moves record-by-record through the array, looking for matches. Because the Select object's `selectedIndex` property is used to define the field number in the `test()` method, you can assume that the index numbers of the options in the Select object and the order of fields in the array are identical. And since the value of the `test()` method is a Boolean `true` or `false`, its use in the `if` statement is to record the value of m (the current record number) in the pointer array when the test is passed by the field being evaluated in the current record.

Note that the pointer array index is incremented by the `counter` variable only after the array receives a data value, and that a value of zero (assigned before the loop) is always the contents of the pointer array's first element—this ensures that the header record (the $0^{th}$ record in the array) will always be displayed as the first record of the output table.

## Outputting Records With the Pointer Array

To output the records passing the search criterion, use the pointer array to order the records of the dynamically-assembled HTML table for output:

```
pointArr = (...a bunch of record numbers...)

var output = "";
for(i = 0; i < pointArr.length; i++)
  {
  output += "<TR>"
  for(j = 0; j < array[pointArr[i]].length; j++)
    {
    output += "<TD>" + array[pointArr[i]][j] + "</TD>"
    }
  output += "</TR>"
  }
document.open();
document.write("<TABLE>");
document.write(output);
document.write("</TABLE>");
document.close();
```

In the example above, the method of creating the HTML table for output is a little different than previously described: the data items and the <TD> and <TR> tags are formed into the HTML table body by concatenating them into a variable named `output`. This variable is then used to output the table body in a series of `document.write()` statements.

The central aspect of crafting the table body is the use of the `i` loop to process through the pointer array, item-by-item, so that the pointer array's data values (the record numbers passing the test) can be used to direct the creation of the table rows in the expression `array[pointArr[i]][j]`.

# TASK 4C-1:

## Coding the Search Functionality

1. In the file displarr.html, **modify the following code:**

   ```
   <FRAMESET COLS="30%,*" FRAMEBORDER="1">
     <FRAME SRC='searchfields.html' NAME='ctrls'>
     <FRAME SRC='blank.html' NAME='results'>
   </FRAMESET>
   ```

   Now the file searchfields.html will load into the left frame of displarr.html.

2. **Save and test your work.** This time, the left frame displays three items:
   - A Button object
   - A Select object
   - A Textbox object

   You will use these items to create single-term, partial-word search functionality for the data table included into searchfields.html.

3. In your editor, **open the file searchfields.html. Locate the following items:**
   - A <SCRIPT> include that pulls in the vino.js file—a data table about wines.
   - A Form object named `MyForm`.
   - A Button object named `SrchBut`.
   - A Select object named `SelObj`.
   - A Textbox object named `SrchTxt`.

   You will work with these items in your coding.

4. In the <HEAD> section of your document, within the <SCRIPT> tags, under the indicated comment, **enter the following code:**

   ```
   function srchflds(selobj)
     {
     var srchRegExp = new RegExp(document.MyForm.SrchTxt.value);
   ```

   This statement instantiates a RegExp object named srchRegExp. Its criterion is defined from the text entered into the SrchTxt textbox by the user.

5. Under the indicated comment, **enter the following code:**

   ```
   // creating the pointer array

     var pointArr = new Array();
     pointArr[0] = 0;
   ```

   This code creates the pointer array and puts the number zero as the value of its first element. Eventually, this array will hold a sequence of record numbers that meet the search criterion.

6. Under the indicated comment, **enter the following code:**

   ```
   // searching through the table to find matches and record
   them in the pointer array

     counter = 1;
     for (m = 1; m < recArr.length; m++)
       {
       if(srchRegExp.test(recArr[m][selobj.selectedIndex]))
         {
         pointArr[counter] = m;
         counter++
         }
       }
   ```

   By using the value held in the `selectedIndex` property of the Select object passed to the function, the code looks at the data values stored in the corresponding data table field as it cycles through the records of the array. For each record, the specified field undergoes a check by the RegExp object's `test()` method. If deemed to meet the criterion of the test, the record number in which the field is located is entered into the pointer array. Notice that the counter variable increments the index number of the pointer array only when matches are made.

7. Under your previous work, **enter the following code:**

```
// outputting the table in search order by using the pointer
array

   var output = "";
   for(i = 0; i < pointArr.length; i++)
     {
     output += "<TR>"
     for(j = 0; j < recArr[pointArr[i]].length; j++)
        {
        output += "<TD>" + recArr[pointArr[i]][j] + "</TD>"
        }
     output += "</TR>"
     }
   top.frames[1].document.open();
   top.frames[1].document.write("<TABLE>");
   top.frames[1].document.write(output);
   top.frames[1].document.write("</TABLE>");
   top.frames[1].document.close();
   }
```

This output code is similar to your previous work, except for one thing. As the outer i loop iterates through the pointer array, the values held in the pointer array are used to construct the table rows. In other words, instead of outputting record 1, record 2, record 3, and so forth, the outer i loop moves through the pointer array, element-by-element, to retrieve its values, which are themselves the sequence of record numbers for output. Those record number values are then used to construct the body of the HTML table.

Let's hook this function up.

8. In the <INPUT> tag for the button, **enter the following code:**

```
<INPUT
 TYPE="button"
 NAME="selbut"
 VALUE="Search on Field"
 onClick="srchflds(document.MyForm.SelObj);">
```

9. **Save and test your work.** When you reload displarr.html, clicking the button without entering any criterion in the text box will display all the records in the table. Then, depending upon the criterion you enter, records meeting the criterion will be selected, based on the field you select from the drop-down list.

# Topic 4D

## Sorting Data for Display

The process for sorting records in a data table for display as an HTML table involves:

1. Determining the field to sort on (based on user interaction).
2. Sorting the data values stored under the field name in the data table.
3. Using the new sort order to create a series of record numbers in a pointer array.
4. Using the pointer array to construct a dynamically-assembled HTML table for output.

### Using a Sort Array

To sort a series of data values stored in a data table under a field name, you can use a sort array. A *sort array* is a one-dimensional array that has as its elements the data values of the field being sorted, along with a means of determining the position of the data item in the data table from which it was extracted. Take for example, the following data table stored as a two-dimensional array:

```
phoneArr[0][0] = "Last Name"
phoneArr[0][1] = "First Name"
phoneArr[0][2] = "Street"
phoneArr[0][3] = "Number"

phoneArr[1][0] = "Adams"
phoneArr[1][1] = "Dan"
phoneArr[1][2] = "132 Main Street"
phoneArr[1][3] = "555-1234"

phoneArr[2][0] = "Burgess"
phoneArr[2][1] = "Candi"
phoneArr[2][2] = "234 South Avenue"
phoneArr[2][3] = "555-2435"

phoneArr[3][0] = "Boatwright"
phoneArr[3][1] = "Darryl"
phoneArr[3][2] = "345 Norton Blvd."
phoneArr[3][3] = "555-4567"
```

The series of array elements entered into the sort array by pulling the data items from the table, record-by-record (not including the header record), might look like this:

```
// elements stored in sortArr...

"Adams,1","Burgess,2","Boatwright,3"
```

Note that each data item is of the form "*dataItem, recno*"—namely, the item followed by a comma and the record number it was extracted from.

To sort the sort array, you use the Array object's `sort()` method:

```
sortArr = sortArr.sort();
```

> **sort array:**
> A one-dimensional array that has as its elements the data values of the field being sorted, along with a means of determining the position of the data item in the data table from which it was extracted.

Sorting the array with the `sort()` method and then reassigning the reordered elements back into `sortArr` yields the following ordering:

```
// new ordering in sortArr...

"Adams,1","Boatwright,3","Burgess,2"
```

At this point, the sort has been completed. Now, the trick is to detach the record numbers that have piggy-backed on their associated data items so that they can be gleaned from the sort array and entered into the pointer array. Here's how that's done:

```
var sortStr = sortArr.join();
```

Using the Array object's `join()` method converts the sequence of array elements held within it into one big string, namely:

```
// string value stored in sortStr...

"Adams,1,Boatwright,3,Burgess,2"
```

Then, the String object's `split()` method is used to reassign the data back into the sort array:

```
sortArr = sortStr.split(',');
```

Denoting the comma as the delimiter between the method's parentheses causes the detachment of the record numbers from their associated items:

```
// detached elements of sortArr after split...

"Adams",1,"Boatwright",3,"Burgess",2
```

At this point, `sortArr` has six elements in it instead of the original three.

## Creating the Pointer Array From the Sort Array

Given a sort array ready to yield its correctly-sequenced record numbers reflecting the sort order for the data table, creating a pointer array is now a matter of detecting the numeric values from the sort array and placing them into the pointer array:

Lesson 4: Displaying and Manipulating Data Tables    87

```
// assume sortArr has the following elements:
// "Adams",1,"Boatwright",3,"Burgess",2

pointArr = new Array();
pointArr[0] = 0;
counter = 1;

for(p = 0; p < sortArr.length; p++)
   {
   if(!isNaN(sortArr[p]) && sortArr[p] != "")
     {
     pointArr[counter] = sortArr[p];
     counter++
     }
   }

// pointArr now holds the following elements:
// 0,1,3,2
```

In the code above, the `if` statement checks the values held in the sort array as the `for` loop cycles through its elements. If the value in the sort array is not-not-a-number (in other words, a number) and not an empty string (in case there were blank data items), it must be a number; therefore, the value is placed as an element in the pointer array.

Once the pointer array is created, it can be used in crafting an HTML table body similar to that of the search feature.

## TASK 4D-1:

### Coding the Sort Functionality

1. In the file displarr.html, **modify the following code:**

   ```
   <FRAMESET COLS="30%,*" FRAMEBORDER="1">
     <FRAME SRC='sortfields.html' NAME='ctrls'>
     <FRAME SRC='blank.html' NAME='results'>
   </FRAMESET>
   ```

   Now the file sortfields.html will load into the left frame of displarr.html.

2. **Save and test your work.** This time, the left frame displays two items:
   - A Button object
   - A Select object

   *You'll get an error message, but that's OK—the page will continue to load.*

   You will use these items to create a single-term sorting feature for the data table included into sortfields.html.

3. In your editor, **open the file sortfields.html. Locate the following items:**
   - A `<SCRIPT>` include that pulls in the vino.js file. The file contains a two-dimensional array named `recArr` that contains a data table about wines.
   - A Form object named `MyForm`.

**88** JavaScript: Advanced Programming (Second Edition)

- A Button object named `SortBut`.
- A Select object named `SelObj`.

You will work with these items in your coding.

4. In the `<HEAD>` section, under the indicated comment, **enter the following code:**

```
function sortflds(selobj)
  {
  sortArr = new Array();
  counter = 0;

  for(m = 1; m < recArr.length; m++)
    {
    for(n = 0; n < recArr[m].length; n++)
      {
      if(selobj.options[n].selected)
        {
        sortArr[counter] = recArr[m][n] + "," + m;
        counter++
        }
      }
    }
  }
```

Using a technique similar to the select-field functionality you coded earlier, the inner n loop uses the index value of the option selected from the Select object to retrieve the data value for the corresponding field held in each record. When retrieved, the data value has its own record number concatenated to it, with a comma placed in between the data value and the record number. By the time the loops finish iterating, the sort array contains all the data values for the relevant field across the entire table; each data value has the record number from which it came appended to it.

5. Under the indicated comment, **enter the following code:**

```
// sorting the sort array and splitting off record numbers

  sortArr = sortArr.sort();
  sortStr = sortArr.join();
  sortArr = sortStr.split(',')
```

This is the heart of the sorting functionality. Here's how it works:

- The strings are sorted in the sort array with the Array object's `sort()` method. Because each data item being sorted is of the type *fieldvalue,recnum*, the record numbers associated with the data items "piggy-back" along into the new ordering.

- The reordered data items are then turned into a single string via the Array object's `join()` method. At this point, the single string consists of an alternating sequence of data values and record numbers that are all separated by commas.

- The single string is broken back up into individual array elements via the String object's `split()` method. Note that the comma delimiter is specified within the method's parentheses.

The point of all this slicing and dicing is to reorder the record numbers according to the field to be sorted on, and then break them off as independent array elements after the reordering. Then, they can be used to construct the pointer array.

6. Under the indicated comment, **enter the following code:**

```
// creating the pointer array from the sort array

    pointArr = new Array();
    pointArr[0] = 0;
    counter = 1;

    for(p = 0; p < sortArr.length; p++)
      {
      if(!isNaN(sortArr[p]) && sortArr[p] != "")
        {
        pointArr[counter] = sortArr[p];
        counter++
        }
      }
```

Basically, this code hunts through the data in the sort array from start to finish to find the record numbers; then it deposits the record numbers into the pointer array. The pointer array is now ready to be used to generate the body of the HTML table for output. Note that an if statement rejects all the non-numeric and empty string data values from the sort array as it gleans the record numbers for use in the pointer array. Note also that the counter variable increments only after a new element has been placed in the pointer array.

7. Under the `// outputting the table in sort order by using the pointer array` comment, **review the entered code.** You'll find that it is identical to the output code you entered for the sorting functionality, in that it uses the pointer array to order the records in the HTML table's body. Let's hook this function up to test your work.

8. In the <INPUT> tag for the Button object, **enter the following code:**

```
<INPUT
 TYPE="button"
 NAME="SortBut"
 VALUE="Sort on Field"
 onClick="sortflds(document.MyForm.SelObj);">
```

9. **Save and test your work.** You should be able to select a field name from the drop-down list, and watch the records order (and reorder) the table generated after you select different sort fields and press the Sort On Field button.

## Summary

In this lesson, you loaded data into code that manipulates data tables, both in hard-coded and delimited file form; then you constructed functionality that selects, sorts, and searches data tables for display on a Web page.

## Lesson Review

**4A** What are the three main activities on which data table manipulation is based?

**4B** What is the impact of using identical index numbers for the fields listed in the Select object of a data table selecting function, and the field ordering of the data table housed in a two-dimensional array used to manipulate the table?

**4C** How is a pointer array used in crafting a single-term search function?

**4D** How can you use a temporary sort array to sort a data table?

YOUR NOTES:

# Cookies

## LESSON 5

## Overview

Computer users expect to be able to customize applications. Window arrangements, display fonts, lists of the most recently used documents—these are just a few of the many customizable settings that users take for granted. On the Macintosh, user preferences are generally stored in the Preferences folder. On the Windows platform, user preferences are stored in .ini files or in the Registry. Other operating systems provide other means for storing such settings.

With Web programming, the ability to save settings semi-permanently is even more important. When users move from page to page, browsers forget variables and objects from previous pages. For this reason, it is important that JavaScript have some way to store data. Although JavaScript is largely prevented from accessing a user's local storage for security reasons, JavaScript does have limited access to a special type of local storage called cookies.

In this lesson, you'll learn how to create, use, and delete cookies.

## Objectives

To create and use your own cookies, you will:

**5A** **Explain why cookies are beneficial, list practical uses for cookies, and explain limitations of cookies.**

You will learn why cookies are necessary. You will also discuss various uses for and limitations of cookies.

**5B** **Write JavaScript statements to store a value within a cookie.**

You will learn how to store cookies, and you will examine an example of a cookie-writing function.

**5C** **Write JavaScript statements to retrieve a value from a cookie, and write statements to store and retrieve multiple values using a single cookie.**

You will then learn about various functions that are useful to know when writing scripts that manage cookies. You will look at some sample cookie-writing functions.

**5D** **Write JavaScript statements to delete a cookie.**

You will learn how to delete a cookie, and what happens when a cookie is deleted. You will also look at an example of a cookie-deleting function.

**Data Files**
*Default.htm*
*Explore\Cookies\*
*Cookies.htm*
*Explore\Cookies\Why.htm*
*Explore\Cookies\Why2.htm*
*Explore\LMSite\LMHome.htm*
*Explore\LMSite\CatFrame.htm*
*Explore\LMSite\CartFrame.htm*
*Explore\Cookies\Store.htm*
*Explore\Cookies\Retrieve.htm*
*Explore\Cookies\Delete.htm*
*Lab - Cookies\Solution\LMHome.htm*
*Lab - Cookies\Solution\Cart.htm*
*Lab - Cookies\Solution\shipping.htm*
*Lab - Cookies\shipping.htm*
*Lab - Cookies\HomeLogo.htm*
*Lab - Cookies\LMHome.htm*
*Lab - Cookies\Cart.htm*

**Lesson Time**
*1 hour, 30 minutes*

# Topic 5A

## Introduction to the Cookie Object

When JavaScript code creates variables and objects, they exist in memory only as long as the page that created them is still loaded. As soon as you move to another page, the browser performs garbage collection and removes them from memory. If you want to carry a value across pages, you need to devise some sort of caching scheme. The most common such scheme is to store the value in a *cookie*.

A cookie is a small chunk of string data stored on a Web client's local disk. The Windows version of Navigator stores cookies in a single file in a subdirectory off the directory that holds the Navigator program. The Macintosh version of Navigator stores cookies in a folder beneath the Preferences folder, in a single file called MagicCookie. The Macintosh and Windows versions of Internet Explorer store each cookie as a separate file in a Cookies folder that is stored within the system folder.

> **cookie:**
> A small chunk of string data that is stored in a Web client's local disk storage. Cookies are typically used to hold user preferences or special data that needs to be maintained across multiple Web pages.

## TASK 5A-1:

### Experimenting With the Lifetime of Variables and Examining a Cookie-based Shopping Cart

**Objective:** To observe how variables behave when you move among Web pages; to consider how cookies can be used to address some of the limitations of variables; and to examine a typical way in which cookies can be used—to hold a user's selections in a shopping cart.

1. **Open the JavaScript Exploratorium.**

2. From the Exploratorium's main menu, **click on Cookies to display a list of links related to cookies.** First, we will explore why cookies are needed.

3. **Click on Why Cookies Are Needed.** The following page is displayed. You will use this page to experiment with a simple variable.

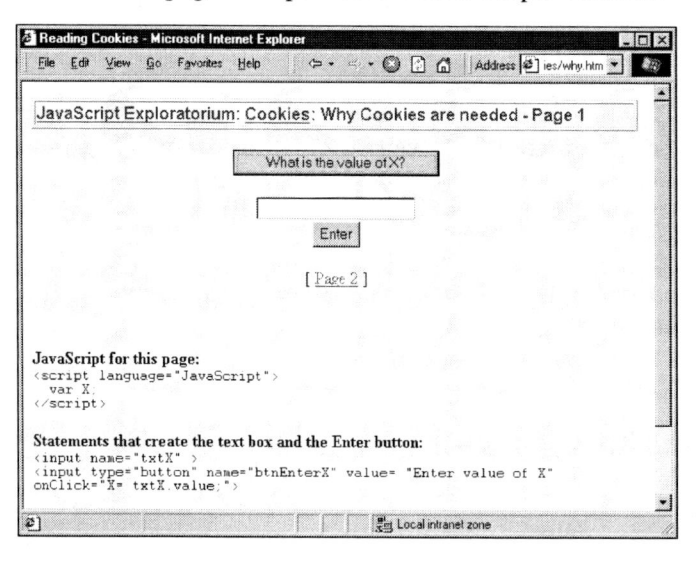

4. In the text box, **enter your name and click the Enter button.**

5. **Click the What Is The Value Of X? button.** An alert box informs you that X is your name. **Click OK.**

6. **Examine the code listings at the bottom of the Web page.**

   ```
   JavaScript for this page:
   <script language="JavaScript">
     var X;
   </script>

   Statements that create the text box and the Enter button:
   <input name="txtX" >
   <input type="button" name="btnEnterX" value= "Enter value of
   X" onClick="X=txtX.value;">

   Statement that creates the "What is the value of X?" button:
   <input type="button" name="btnWhatX" value="What is the value
   of X?" onClick="alert('X is ' + X)">
   ```

   The JavaScript for this page is very simple. It declares a variable called X. Because X is declared outside a function, it is global. In other words, X is available to every function in the page and will not be destroyed after functions finish running. The click event (onClick) for the Enter button runs a simple statement that copies the value that is in the text box into the variable X.

   The click event for the bottom button simply displays the value of X in an alert box.

7. **Consider the code listing.** If you move to another page or exit the browser, will the value of X still be available to you? Will variables associated with a particular page retain their value when you return to that page? Let's experiment to find out the answers to these questions.

8. **Click the Page 2 link.** Page 2 is similar to Page 1, except that it does not have the text box and button that you used to enter the value of X.

9. **Click the What Is The Value Of X? button.** An alert box informs you that X is undefined. **Click OK.**

   Consider what will happen if you return to Page 1. Is X associated with that page and still in memory? Or was it erased when you moved to Page 2?

10. **Click on the Page 1 link and click the What Is The Value Of X? button.** As it turns out, X is still undefined.

    **Click OK** to dismiss the message box.

As you can see, variables are kept in memory, but are destroyed as soon as you leave a page. Even if you return to the original page, the original contents of the variable will not be in memory.

11. **Return to the main menu of the JavaScript Exploratorium.**

    Consider solutions to the problem that you experienced in the previous task. How might you carry a value from one page to another? How might you store values so that they persist after the user exits the browser?

    To protect the security of Web users, JavaScript cannot directly access files stored on a user's local disk drive. Therefore, the solution to this problem is not as simple as it might be.

    There are a number of solutions—or at least workarounds. For example, you could use a frames page and declare your variables within a frame that does not go away when you move from page to page. Of course, this means that you might have to use frames in situations where you have no other reason for using them. You could have an invisible frame (whose height, for example, is set to 0), but that approach could get cumbersome. Other solutions are awkward or unmanageable, requiring a specific browser version or the use of applets or plug-ins that some users might object to having on their computers.

    The most common solution, as you've probably figured out by this lesson's title, is to use cookies to store data on the user's local hard drive. In the next task, we'll examine a typical use of cookies—to hold items in an online shopping cart, such as the one shown in Figure 5-1 below:

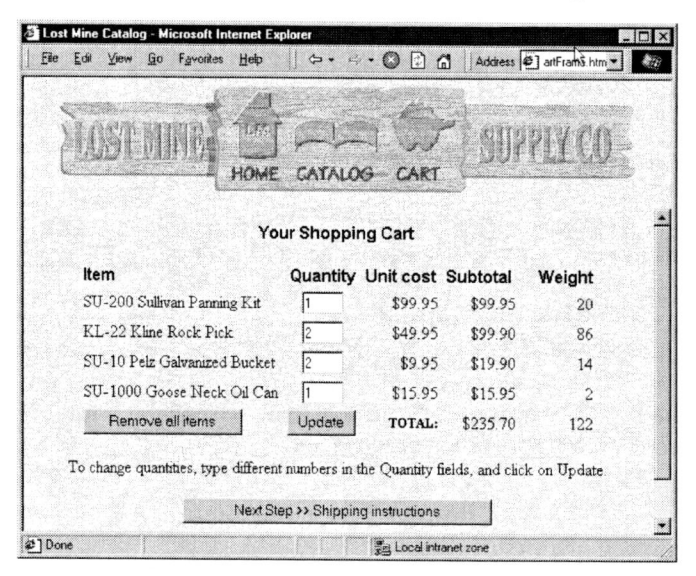

**Figure 5-1:** *A cookie-based shopping cart.*

12. **From the JavaScript Exploratorium's main menu, click Lost Mine Web Site Demo.** The welcome page for the Lost Mine Supply Company is displayed.

13. **Click on Catalog.** A product catalog will be displayed momentarily. The catalog consists of a list of items with a product description and a picture of each product. Near the top of the screen are links to move between the catalog and the shopping cart.

96   *JavaScript: Advanced Programming (Second Edition)*

14. **Click on Cart.** Unless you have already experimented with the online catalog, the cart should be empty. Let's add some items to the cart.

15. **Click on Catalog.** Beneath each picture is a link labeled "Add to cart." **Click on one of the links.** You are prompted to enter the number of items you wish to buy. You can leave the default value of 1, or you can enter an amount. (Do so now.)

16. **Click OK** to add the item to your order. If you'd like, order a few other items. (Don't worry; this is a simulation. You won't actually place an order!)

17. **Click on Cart.** A summary of the items you ordered is displayed.

18. **Exit the browser application, and then return to the Lost Mine Web Site Demo.** (The link is in the main menu of the JavaScript Exploratorium.) **Click on Cart.** The items you ordered are still in the shopping cart. **Exit the browser application.**

## Other Practical Uses for Cookies

In addition to allowing online shopping cart functionality, cookies have many other practical uses. For example, you might design a Web site that enables users to select the content that they see, or how it is displayed. Suppose, for example, you were building the home page for an Internet service provider or a Web portal (like **yahoo.com** or **elementk.com**). You could enable users to choose which stocks are displayed within a stock ticker, or what parts of the world they would like weather reports for. Preferences such as these could be stored in a cookie.

## Limitations

You should use cookies for fairly small amounts of data that you intend to access infrequently. The specification for cookies limits how much storage they can consume on a user's hard disk drive. Your cookie files can contain no more than 300 total cookies, and no more than 20 for a single Web server or domain name. Once the limit is reached, cookies may be automatically deleted, beginning with the oldest and working toward the youngest.

These facts encourage the Web developer to combine multiple bits of data into a single cookie. However, you should bear in mind that each cookie can contain no more than 4,096 characters, according to the specification. In practice, the real limit may be as small as half that amount. Characters that exceed the maximum are simply truncated from the file.

## Topic 5B

### Storing Cookies

Cookies are stored by writing values to the Document object's Cookie property. To give the current page a temporary cookie, set the `document.cookie` property to a string such as:

```
document.cookie = "myCookie=gingerbread";
```

If the browser detects no cookie with the specified name, it creates one. If a cookie by that name already exists, the browser replaces it with the new one. The above name/value pair would be stored in the cookie as `myCookie=gingerbread`.

### Using the escape( ) Function to Encode Cookie Values

As you can see above, the entire cookie is a string. If you have multiple cookies, they are separated by semicolons. For this reason, you can't include semicolons within the cookie's value field, nor can you use commas and spaces. However, you can use JavaScript's `escape()` function to encode such special characters in values that you want to save in a cookie, as in the following example:

```
cookieValue = escape("Ginger Snaps, baked until rock hard");
document.cookie = "myCookie=" + cookieValue;
```

The escape function in the first statement assigns the following string to `cookieValue`:

```
Ginger%20Snaps%2C%20baked%20until%20rock%20hard
```

The `escape()` function converts special characters (in this example, the comma and spaces) into a percent symbol followed by a hexadecimal number that represents the Latin-1 code for that character. Hexadecimal is a numbering system based on the 16 digits 0, 1, 2, 3, 4, 5, 6, 7, 8, 9, A, B, C, D, E, and F—rather than the 10 digits of our normal base-10 system. Latin-1 is a character-encoding scheme that uses numbers to represent characters. It was designed to be portable across a wide variety of computer systems and networks.

Fortunately, you don't need to know how to read hexadecimal or Latin-1 encoding. When you retrieve a string that was encoded by the `escape()` function, you can use the `unescape()` function to decode the string back into normal text, as in the following example:

```
somethingHumansCanRead = unescape(encodedCookieString);
```

### Assigning Cookies an Expiration Date

The Name and Value fields are required for creating a cookie. However, there are several optional fields that you can include as well. One of these is the Expires field. If you do not include an Expires field, cookies that you create might be erased as soon as you exit the browser application. (Navigator consistently purges undated cookies as soon as the browser is exited; Internet Explorer tends to permit undated cookies to hang around for a while.)

To specifically request that the cookie last beyond the current browser session, you need to specify a value in the Expires field, as in the following:

```
expDate = "Wed, 3 Mar 2000 14:41:00 UTC";
document.cookie = "myCookie=sugardrop;" +
                  "expires=" + expDate;
```

The expiration date must be in the Greenwich Mean Time (GMT) string format, as shown above. You can specify the date directly, or you can use JavaScript's Date functions to calculate a date for you. For example, the following statements calculate an expiration date of one year from today:

```
1. today    = new Date();
2. nextYear = new Date();
3. today    = today.getTime();
4. nextYear.setTime(today + 365 * 24 * 60 * 60 * 1000);
5. expDate = nextYear.toGMTString();
```

Lines 1 and 2 create new Date objects to hold today's date and the date one year from today. Line 3 assigns the current date and time to `today`, which was created in line 1. Line 4 sets `nextYear`'s time to today's time, plus 365 days times 24 hours times 60 minutes times 60 seconds times 1000 milliseconds. This calculation doesn't take leap years into account (or continental drift, for that matter), but it's close enough for this purpose. Line 5 converts `nextYear`'s date value into a GMT string that can be used as a cookie expiration date.

## Assigning a Path and Domain

The Domain field enables you to specify the domain (for example, **www.elementk.com** or **rochester.rr.com**) with which a cookie is associated. You can use the Path field to specify what URLs within that domain are associated with the cookie. This enables you to be very specific about which servers or Web pages can access a particular cookie.

## The Domain Field

When a request is made to read a cookie, the browser compares the domain field of the cookie against the domain name of the Web page running the JavaScript. A match is found by reading from right to left. In other words, a cookie with a domain attribute of fenster.com could be read by Web page script hosted on fenster.com, windows.fenster.com, and home.fenster.com—but not fenster.windows.com.

Hosts (for our purposes, that would be Web pages containing JavaScript) that set a cookie's domain must be within that domain themselves. For example, JavaScript running on the Web page `www.fenster.com/bakery.htm` cannot set a cookie to have the domain `www.elementk.com`.

There are also rules regarding the number of periods that must fall within a domain. Domains that end with one of the Top Seven levels (`.com`, `.edu`, `.org`, `.gov`, `.mil`, `.net`, and `.int`) must have at least two periods (for example, **www.nasa.gov** or **www.maccoplastics.com**—but not **maccoplastics.com**). All others must have at least three periods (for example, **www.fenco.com.jp** or **www.ozfenster.com.au**—but not **ozfenster.com.au**).

If you omit the domain field when you write a cookie, the domain of the server that hosts the Web page is used. Usually, the default setting works just fine.

## The Path Field

The path field identifies which URLs within the specified domain can access the cookie. The path is evaluated similarly to the domain, except that it is performed from left to right. For example, a cookie with the path attribute /chow could be read by JavaScripts in documents such as /chowsang/home.htm or /chow/recipes.htm, but not /dogchow/recipes.htm.

If you omit the Path field, the path of the Web page that contains the JavaScript is used. Again, the default setting is usually fine.

## The Secure Field

If you include the Secure attribute when you write a cookie, the cookie can only be accessed if the host calling for it (for example, a Web page containing JavaScript that reads a cookie) is running over a secure connection (such as that provided by the HTTPS (HTTP running on SSL) protocol. By omitting this, any host that passes the criteria specified by the domain and path fields can access the cookie.

## A Sample Function That Stores a Value in a Cookie

The following is an example of a function that stores a value in a cookie. This function accepts six arguments that correspond to the cookie fields described above. Only the first two arguments (cName and cValue) are required.

```
1. function setCookie(cName,cValue,eDate,cPath⇒
,cDomain,cSecurity) {
2.    var theCookie = cName + "=" + escape(cValue);
3.    if (eDate)      theCookie += ";expires=" + eDate;
4.    if (cPath)      theCookie += ";path=" + cPath;
5.    if (cDomain)    theCookie += ";domain=" + cDomain;
6.    if (cSecurity)  theCookie += ";secure";
7.    document.cookie = theCookie;
8. }
```

Line 1 accepts the six arguments, assigning them to the local variables listed. Line 2 places the cookie name and value into a string called theCookie. The cookie name and value are separated by an equals sign. The value is encoded through a call to the escape() function. If an expiration date was specified, line 3 adds a semicolon to separate the Expires field from the name and value, along with "expires=" and the expiration date. Similar to line 3, lines 4, 5, and 6 add the specified fields if they are provided to the setCookie function. Line 7 writes the cookie, using the cookie string that was constructed by the previous lines.

# TASK 5B-1:

## Examining a Cookie-writing Function

**Objective:** To explore how cookies are written by examining a cookie-writing function.

1. **Open the JavaScript Exploratorium's main menu** in your Web browser.

2. **Click on Cookies.** A list of topics related to cookies is displayed. **Click on Storing Cookies.** The following page is displayed.

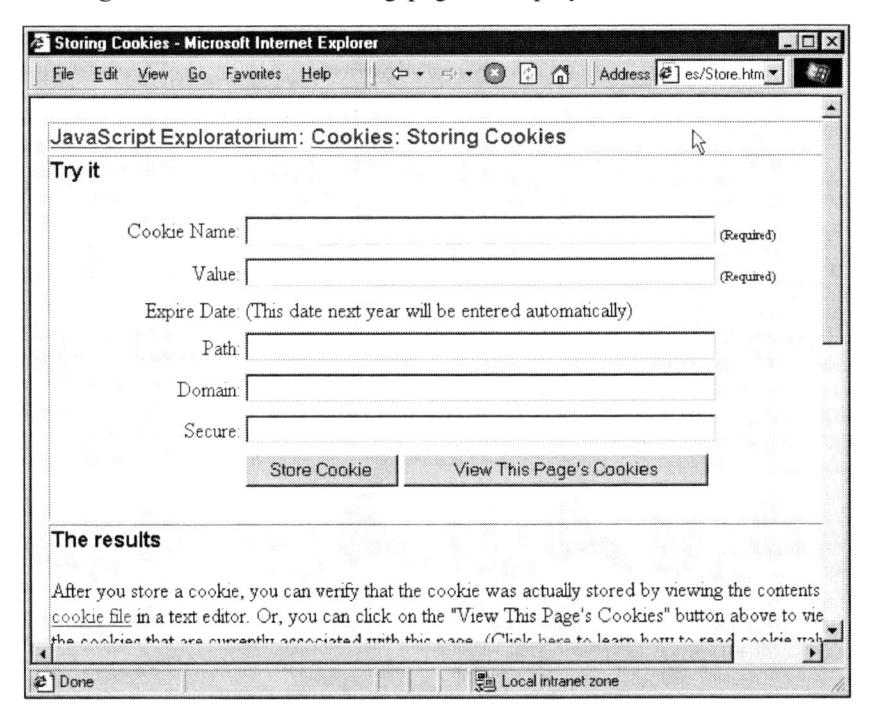

3. **Click on View This Page's Cookies.** Unless you have already been experimenting with this page, an empty JavaScript alert box should appear. It's empty because this page has no cookies. **Click OK** to dismiss the alert box.

4. Now let's store a cookie. In the Cookie Name text box, **type *userName*.** In the Value text box, **type your name. Click on Store Cookie.** Although nothing appeared to happen, your cookie was stored.

5. Let's verify that your cookie was stored. **Click on View This Page's Cookies.** The cookie string is displayed, in the "name=value" format, as shown below. **Click on OK** to dismiss the alert box.

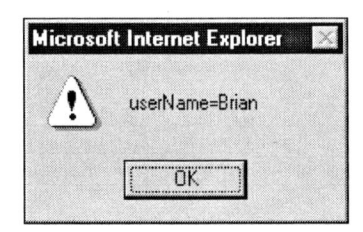

6. Let's add another cookie. **Change the text in the Cookie Name text box to** *userAge*. **Enter your age** (make one up if you'd like) in the Value text box. **Click on Store Cookie.**

Lesson 5: Cookies    101

7. Now let's see what this page's cookies look like. **Click on View This Page's Cookies.** The two cookies you entered are displayed in the "name=value" format, separated by a semicolon, as shown below. **Click OK** to dismiss the alert box.

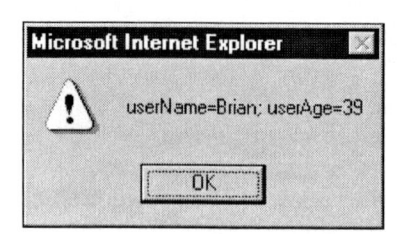

> Microsoft Internet Explorer
> userName=Brian; userAge=39
> OK

8. Now let's change the value of the first cookie. **Change the text in the Cookie Name text box to *userName*.** In the Value text box, **type *Sam Patch* and click on Store Cookie.**

9. Now **click on View This Page's Cookies.** The userName cookie should now be assigned the value "Sam Patch." **Click OK** to dismiss the alert box.

> Microsoft Internet Explorer
> userName=Sam Patch; userAge=39
> OK

10. **Exit your browser application, and reopen the JavaScript Exploratorium. Click on Cookies, then click on Storing Cookies** to return to the page where you wrote the cookies. **Click on View This Page's Cookies.** Although you have exited the browser and moved from page to page, you have not lost your cookies.

11. **Click OK and exit your browser application.**

# Topic 5C

## Reading and Processing Cookie Values

As you saw in the previous task, all of the cookies for a single document are stored as a single string, with cookies separated by semicolons. Retrieving cookies is fairly simple; you simply read the `Cookies` property of the Document object. For example, the Storing Cookies page of the JavaScript Exploratorium uses the following two statements to show you the current cookie content for the document:

```
var cookieString = document.cookie;
alert(unescape(CookieString));
```

As you can see, reading all of the cookies at once is a simple matter; however, extracting a value from one cookie takes a bit of processing.

## Dividing Up the Cookie String

Once you have a string containing all of the cookies, you then need to extract the cookie you want to read. Semicolons separate cookies in the cookie string. To divide the string into separate cookies, you simply need to split the cookie string up where the semicolons appear. An array is a convenient way to work with a list of similar items like cookies, so we'll look at two ways to divide the cookie string up into an array, in which each element will contain one cookie in the "name=value" format.

## The split() Method

Since version 3.0 of Navigator and version 4 of Internet Explorer, the String object has had a `split()` method, which splits up a string into an array of strings. You pass the `split()` method a delimiter character that specifies where to split the string up. Consider the illustration below:

If: cookieString = uName=Fred;uAge=52

then this statement: cookieArray = cookieString.split(";");

creates this array:
cookieArray[0] = uName=Fred
cookieArray[1] = uAge=52

**Figure 5-2:** Using the `split()` method to split the cookie string into an array.

The `split()` method is simple and effective, but if you need to support older browsers, you'll need another approach. One approach is to build an equivalent to the `split()` method by using the `indexOf()`, `substring()`, and `length()` methods.

## The indexOf(), substring(), and length() Methods

You can combine the `indexOf()`, `substring()`, and `length()` methods (all of which belong to the String object) to perform some heavy-duty string manipulation.

The `indexOf()` method returns the location of one string within another. For example, the expression `cookieString.indexOf(";")` returns the location of the first semicolon in cookieString. If cookieString contains `"uName=Fred;uAge=52,"` then `cookieString.indexOf(";")` would return the value 10, as you can see in the following illustration:

| 0 | 1 | 2 | 3 | 4 | 5 | 6 | 7 | 8 | 9 | 10 | 11 | 12 | 13 | 14 | 15 | 16 | 17 |
|---|---|---|---|---|---|---|---|---|---|----|----|----|----|----|----|----|----|
| u | N | a | m | e | = | F | r | e | d | ;  | u  | A  | g  | e  | =  | 5  | 2  |

**Figure 5-3:** Using `indexOf()` to find the end of the first cookie.

The `length()` method returns the length of the string. The `substring()` method extracts one string from another, based on the locations passed to it. Let's see how `indexOf()`, `substring()`, and `length()` can be used together to create an equivalent to the `split()` method. Examine the following code:

```
1.  // Return an array of strings from
2.  // a character-delimited string
3.  function split(delimiter, s) {
4.     theArray = new Array();
5.     while (s != "") {
6.        endOfChunk = s.indexOf(delimiter);
7.        if (endOfChunk == -1) endOfChunk = s.length;
8.        var thisChunk = s.substring(0,endOfChunk);
9.        s = s.substring(endOfChunk+1,s.length);
10.         theArray[theArray.length] = thisChunk;
11.    }
12.    return theArray;
13. }
```

This function takes a string argument (`"s"`) in addition to the delimiter. The string argument specifies the string that you want to translate into an array of strings. The delimiter, of course, specifies which character delimits the items in the original string.

In line 4, the function creates a new array to hold the strings. Line 5 begins a `while` loop that performs a series of statements on the string "s" until it is empty. Line 6 finds the end of the first substring by locating the first instance of the delimiter character. If the delimiter character is not found, line 7 finds the end of the entire string, in which case, we have found the last substring in the array. Line 8 extracts the substring up to the delimiter, and line 9 subtracts the substring from the original string. Line 10 assigns the substring to the next item in the array. If the string is not empty, execution returns to line 6, at the top of the `while` loop. If the string is empty, then the array is returned as the result of the function. To obtain an array containing the `"name=value"` pairs for every cookie associated with a document, you could call the `split()` function as follows:

```
var cookieString = document.cookie;
cookieArray = split(";", cookieString);
```

## Reading a Specific Cookie

There are many ways to extract cookies by using the string functions we've looked at. Once you have separated the cookies (into an array or a variable), you'll need to find the specific cookie you want to read. Using the array returned by our custom `split()` function or the String object's `split()` method, it is fairly simple to loop through the array to find the cookie you want to read. The following is a simple example of how this might be done:

```
1.  // getCookie retrieves data from the named cookie
2.  function getCookie(cName) {
3.    if (cName) {
4.      cookieArray = split(";",document.cookie);
5.      for (i=0; i<cookieArray.length; i++) {
6.        aCookie = cookieArray[i];
7.        if (aCookie.indexOf(cName+"=") > -1) {
8.          var valueLoc = aCookie.indexOf("=")+1;
9.          cookieValue = ⇒
            aCookie.substring(valueLoc,aCookie.length);
10.         return unescape(cookieValue);
11.       }
12.     }
13.   }
14.   return false;
15. }
```

Line 3 determines whether this function has been passed a cookie name. If it has not, then the cookie is not processed. The function simply returns `false` (line 14).

If a cookie name has been passed to the function, then line 4 copies the cookie's contents into an array of strings, separating elements where there are semicolons.

The `for` loop in lines 5 through 12 then searches each array element, to see if its contents begin with the name of the cookie, followed immediately by an equals sign (line 7). If so, then the cookie specified by `cName` has been found. Lines 8 and 9 then extract the part of the cookie following the equals sign. This is the value of the cookie, which is returned to the calling statement in line 10. The value is unescaped to convert escape characters.

If the loop ends without finding the specified cookie, line 14 returns `false` to the calling statement.

## Storing Multiple Items in a Single Cookie

Given the limitations on the number of cookies available to you, it might be necessary to store multiple items in a single cookie. Just as multiple cookies are separated in the cookie string by a semicolon, you can use a delimiter character to separate multiple values within a single cookie. Because you already have a `split()` function, separating such values is a simple task. Characters that make good delimiters within cookies include the colon (":") and comma (","). As with the semicolon cookie delimiter, you'll need to have a way to encode those characters when they are part of the content itself, or else use a delimiter that you know will never be in the cookie content.

Let's see how this works. Suppose you have a cookie named `partsSelected` that contains a list of parts that a user has selected from inventory. You could add a newly-selected part to the `partsSelected` cookie as shown below:

```
1.  partsList = getCookie(partsSelected);
2.  if (partsList != "") partsList += ":";
3.  partsList += newPartToAdd;
4.  setCookie(partsSelected,partsList);
```

Line 1 gets the current parts list from the cookie. If the list already contains at least one part, Line 2 adds a colon to the end of the list to separate the new part from the rest of the list. Line 3 adds the new part to the end of the list. Line 4 writes the updated list to the cookie.

# TASK 5C-1:

## Examining Cookie-reading Functions

**Objective:** To explore how cookies are retrieved by examining and using cookie-reading functions.

1. **Display the Cookies page** of the JavaScript Exploratorium.

2. Before we examine some cookie-reading functions, let's add another cookie. **Click on Storing Cookies.**

3. In the Cookie Name text box, **type numberOfChildren.** In the Value text box, **type 7. Click on Store Cookie.** Now let's add yet another cookie. In this one, we'll store several values.

4. In the Cookie Name text box, **type *agesOfChildren*.** In the Value text box, **type *2:4:5:8:10:13:18*.** (We've separated the values with colons.) **Click on Store Cookie.**

5. Now let's see what this page's cookies look like. **Click on View This Page's Cookies.** If you stored other cookies in earlier tasks, they appear in the list along with the new cookies you just made. Observe how the semicolon separates the cookies, and the colon separates values within a single cookie. **Click OK** to dismiss the alert box.

```
Microsoft Internet Explorer                          [X]

  !   userName=Sam Patch; userAge=39; numberOfChildren=7;
      agesOfChildren=2:4:5:8:10:13:18

              [    OK    ]
```

6. Now let's read the cookie values back. At the top of the page, **click on Cookies.** This link will return you to the main cookies page.

**106** JavaScript: Advanced Programming (Second Edition)

7. **Click on Reading Cookies.** In the Cookie Name text box, **type** *agesOfChildren*. **Click on Read Cookie.** The alert box displays just the contents of the agesOfChildren cookie, as shown below. **Click OK** to dismiss the alert box.

   [Microsoft Internet Explorer alert: "The value of agesOfChildren is 2:4:5:8:10:13:18"]

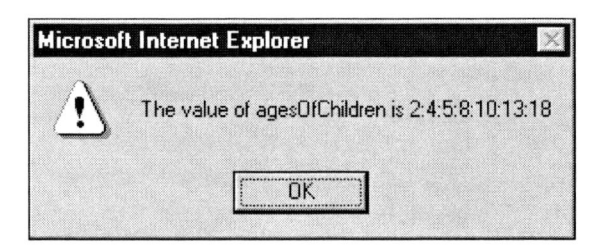

8. Now let's view just the first value from agesOfChildren. **Click on Read First Element (colon-delimited).** The age "2" was extracted from the list by using the split function. **Click OK** to dismiss the alert box.

   [Microsoft Internet Explorer alert: "2 is the first element in the list 2:4:5:8:10:13:18."]

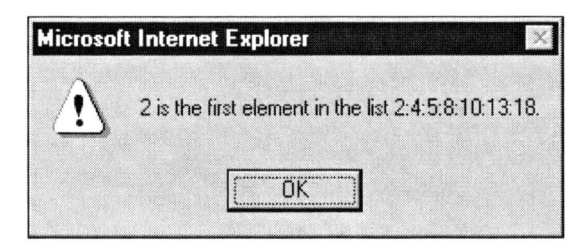

   The function that extracted the first element is shown below. **Exit the browser application.**

```
function demoReadOne() {
  var theCookie =
getCookie(document.frmReadCookie.fldName.value);
  if (theCookie) {
    ageArray = split(":", theCookie);
    alert(ageArray[0] + " is the first element in the list " +
        theCookie + ".");
  } else {
    alert("That cookie was not found");
  }
}
```

# Topic 5D

## Deleting Cookies

Cookies are deleted automatically by the Web browser according to their expiration date. Because you assign an expiration date by writing to a cookie, the code for deleting a cookie looks similar to that for writing to a cookie. To delete a cookie, simply write a new (arbitrary) value to the cookie, assigning it an expiration date before the current date. The browser will take care of the rest. An example function is shown in the following:

```
// KillCookie deletes a cookie
function KillCookie (cookieName, cookiePath, cookieDomain) {
  var theCookie = cookieName + "=";
  if (cookiePath) theCookie += "; path=" + cookiePath;
  if (cookieDomain) theCookie += "; domain=" + cookieDomain;
  theCookie += "; expires=Thu, 01-Jan-70 00:00:01 GMT";
  document.cookie = theCookie;
}
```

In this example, an expiration date of January 1, 1970 is assigned as the cookie's expiration date. This is the oldest date that the browser can read. Setting the cookie's date back so far in time (at least as measured in Internet years) ensures that it will be deleted as soon as the browser gets around to discarding old cookies.

## TASK 5D-1:

### Examining a Cookie-deleting Function

**Objective:** In this activity, you will explore how cookies are deleted by examining a cookie-deleting function in the JavaScript Exploratorium.

1. **Display the Cookies page** of the JavaScript Exploratorium. **Click on Deleting Cookies.**

2. **Click on View This Page's Cookies** to verify that there are cookies left over from previous tasks that you have performed.

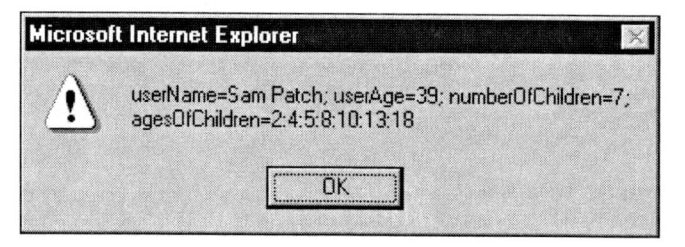

3. **Observe the name of at least one of the cookies associated with this page** (agesOfChildren, for example). If there are no cookies associated with this page, then you'll need to use the Storing Cookies page in the JavaScript Exploratorium to create some before you move on to step 4. **Click OK** to dismiss the alert box.

4. In the Cookie Name text box, **enter the name of the cookie that you want to delete.** Make sure that you capitalize it correctly. **Click on Delete Cookie.** A message informs you that the cookie has been marked for deletion.

108  JavaScript: Advanced Programming (Second Edition)

**Click OK.**

5. **Click on View This Page's Cookies.** The cookie that you marked for deletion is either empty (if you are running Internet Explorer) or gone (if you are running Navigator). If it has not been deleted yet, it will be deleted when the browser purges old cookies.

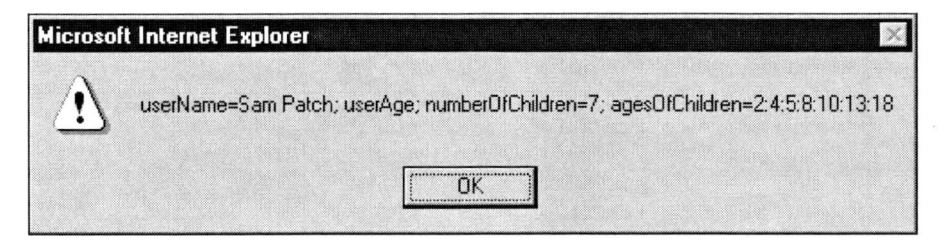

> Microsoft Internet Explorer
>
> ⚠ userName=Sam Patch; userAge; numberOfChildren=7; agesOfChildren=2:4:5:8:10:13:18
>
> [ OK ]

**Click OK.**

6. **Exit the browser.**

# Apply Your Knowledge 5-1

**Suggested Time:**
*15 minutes*

## Storing a User Name in a Cookie

In this activity, you will enable a partially-finished online shopping catalog to save a users' name using a cookie.

1. In the JavaScript Adv Prog folder, open the folder Lab - Cookies. This folder contains a copy of the Lost Mine Web Site in which some of the cookie functionality is not finished. You will add the cookie functionality in this practice lab by adding code to HomeLogo.htm and shipping.htm.

2. Open the folder Solution. This contains a finished version of the project.

3. Open LMHome.htm in your Web browser. (Make sure you're still in the Solution folder.) The greeting at the top of the page says "Welcome, miner!"

4. Click on Cart. The shopping cart is displayed.

5. Click on Next Step→Shipping Instructions. A form is provided for entering your name.

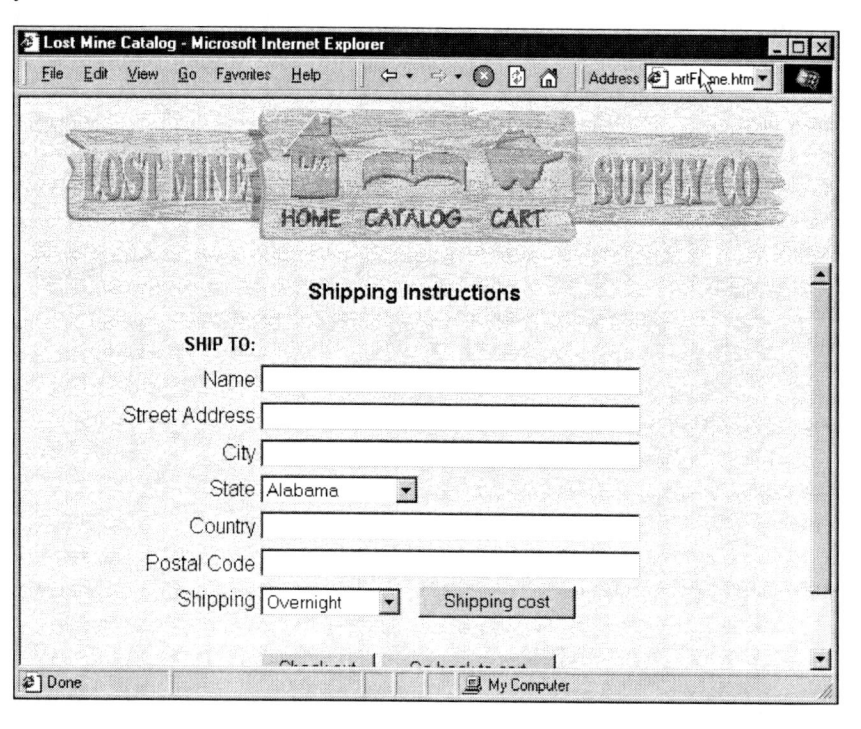

6. Enter your name in the Name text box. When you leave this text box, your name will be written to a cookie.

7. Press Tab. This moves you to the next field. Your name should have been written to a cookie at this point. Let's verify that it was.

8. Click on Home. The greeting now says "Welcome back" with your name, as you entered it in the shipping form. This message will greet you the next time you return to this page, because it was stored in a cookie with an expiration date one year from now.

9. Exit your browser application.

10. Return to the Lab - Cookies folder (not the Solution folder). This folder contains several files that make up the Web site, including two that you will need to change to add the cookie functionality that you just observed.

11. Shipping.htm is the page that contains the shipping form in which you entered your name. A script tag is already in shipping.htm to include the code from cookies.js, so you can use the functions (getCookie and setCookie) in that file. Make the following additions to the code in shipping.htm. Both additions will require you to refer to the contents of the Name text box. The Name text box is document.frmAddress.txtName.

    - Write code for the setName function. SetName runs when the page loads. When setName runs, it should read a cookie called userName. If userName exists (if getCookie does not return False when attempting to read userName), then the value of document.frmAddress.txtName should be set to the value of userName. This will automatically put the user's name into the shipping form's Name text box if the name has been saved in a cookie.

    - Write code for the storeName function. StoreName runs when the user has entered a new name in the Name text box. When storeName runs, it should store the value of the Name text box in a cookie called userName. The cookie should be set to expire one year from today.

12. Modify HomeLogo.htm. This document contains the greeting screen for the Web site. It contains a script that writes a welcome message. If it finds the user's name in a cookie called userName, it writes "Welcome back, Joe User!" (or whatever the user's name is). If user's name is not in the userName cookie (The getCookie function in cookies.js returns false if the specified cookie is not found.), it simply writes "Welcome, miner!"

13. Test your modifications by opening LMHome.htm in your Web browser, and performing steps 3 through 7.

## Summary

In this lesson, you learned why cookies are necessary and you discussed various uses for cookies. You learned how to store and delete cookies, and you learned about various functions that are useful to know when writing scripts that manage cookies. Finally, you looked at and analyzed several examples of cookie-management functions.

## Lesson Review

**5A** Briefly explain why cookies are beneficial, and explain their limitations.

**5B** Write an example statement that stores a value within a cookie.

**5C** Briefly describe the approach for reading cookies.

**5D** Briefly describe the approach for deleting cookies.

YOUR NOTES:

# Communicating With Applets

## LESSON 6

## Overview

As new browser versions are released, JavaScript and the object models it accesses become increasingly capable and feature-laden. Still, there are times when it is appropriate to offload processing to applets. This lesson examines basic techniques for communicating with applets.

## Objectives

To communicate between JavaScript and other software, you will:

**6A** **Write HTML tags and JavaScript code to enable two-way communication with a Java applet.**

You will use a sample Java applet to examine how JavaScript communicates with the applet.

**6B** **Write HTML tags and JavaScript code to enable two-way communication with a Shockwave movie.**

You will use a sample Shockwave movie to examine how JavaScript communicates with it.

**6C** **Write HTML tags and JavaScript code to enable two-way communication with an ActiveX control.**

You will use a sample ActiveX control to examine how JavaScript communicates with it.

**Data Files**
*Default.htm*
*Explore\Applets\Applets.htm*
*Explore\Applets\Java\Java.html*
*Explore\Applets\SWave\Shocked.htm*
*Explore\Applets\ActiveX\ActiveX.htm*
*Explore\Applets\CGI.htm*

**Lesson Time**
1 hour, 15 minutes

## Topic 6A

### Communicating With Java Applets

An *applet* is a small program embedded within a Web page, similar to the way an image file can be embedded within a Web page. Although the applet itself is stored in a file separate from the Web page, when it is displayed to the user, it is confined to a rectangle within the page as though it were actually part of the page.

**applet:**
*A small program that is embedded within a Web page. Applets run on client computers, rather than on a Web server.*

Programmers use Java compilers to create applets using the Java programming language. Java applets can perform interactive animations, immediate calculations, or other simple tasks without having to send a user request back to the server.

Java applets are written in a language similar in some regards to JavaScript. However, Java has a different set of capabilities and limitations from JavaScript. Therefore, Java applets are sometimes used to perform tasks that JavaScript cannot perform directly. Java applets can communicate directly with JavaScript. This provides for some interesting extensions to the capabilities of Web pages.

Although this is not a course on Java programming, this topic will introduce you to the Java/JavaScript interface so that you can get an idea of the type of communication that is possible between Java and JavaScript. If you work on a team in which others develop Java applets for you, then hopefully this will give you a better idea of what sorts of applets to ask for. Or if you intend to learn Java programming, this topic might give you a little bit of a headstart.

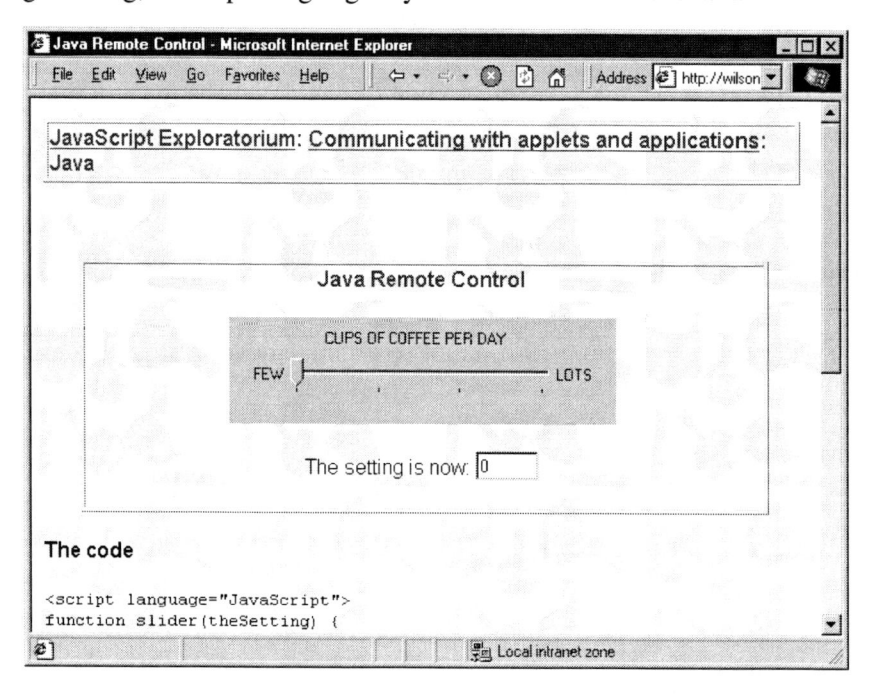

**Figure 6-1:** *A Java applet embedded within a Web page.*

116    JavaScript: Advanced Programming (Second Edition)

# TASK 6A-1:

## Examining a Java Applet

**Objective:** To examine a Java applet that is capable of two-way communication with JavaScript.

**Setup:** You will need a Java-enabled browser.

1. From the JavaScript Exploratorium's main menu, **click on Communicating With Applets And Applications.** A list of applet and application types is displayed.

2. **Click on Java.** Once Java has started, a simple Java applet, a slider control, is displayed.

3. **Drag the slider control to the right.** Examine the change in the "setting" text box. Set the slider to its highest setting. The text box should contain "30" when the slider is all the way to the right.

4. In the space provided below, **list situations in which it might be appropriate to use a Java applet.** If you have seen examples of Java applets other than the one demonstrated in this task, **list them here.**

   _____

   _____

   _____

5. **Share your ideas from step 4 with others in the class, and note additional ideas from other students in the space above.**

6. **Examine the code listing below the applet.** The code is explained in the pages that follow.

## Setting Applet Parameters Through Applet and Param

The following code listing shows how an applet is embedded in a Web page:

```
<APPLET align   = "middle"
        code    = javact1.Slider.class
        archive = ".\slider.jar"
        name    = slider
        height  = 80
        width   = 300
        mayscript >

   <PARAM name="mintitle" value="FEW">
   <PARAM name="maxtitle" value="LOTS">
   <PARAM name="minvalue" value="0">
   <PARAM name="maxvalue" value="30">
   <PARAM name="Title"    value="CUPS OF COFFEE PER DAY">
</APPLET>
```

You embed a Java applet in an HTML document by using the `<APPLET>` `</APPLET>` tag pair. The `<APPLET>` tag accepts the following parameters:

- `code`—the name of the file that contains the applet.
- `archive`—the name of the compressed file that contains the Java applet. If the file specified by `code` is not compressed, then this parameter is not necessary.
- `name`—the name of the applet, as it will be known to the Web page. JavaScript that refers to the applet must use this name.
- `height`—the height of the applet, in pixels, that will be displayed in the Web page.
- `width`—the width of the applet, in pixels.
- `mayscript`—indicates that the Applet can be scripted by JavaScript (or other scripting languages such as VBScript). You must include `mayscript` if you intend to provide interaction between the applet and JavaScript.

Additional parameters (such as custom parameters defined for the applet by the Java programmer) can be passed using Param tags. In the example above, the parameters `mintitle`, `maxtitle`, `minvalue`, `maxvalue`, and `setting` are passed using Param tags. By providing customizable settings in an applet, you can use a single applet for a wide variety of purposes.

## Providing Interactivity Between an Applet and JavaScript

There are several ways to pass information to JavaScript from a Java applet. Perhaps the simplest approach is to use the Java class `netscape.javascript.JSObject`, which is implemented through Netscape's LiveConnect interface. `JSObject` is also supported in Internet Explorer 4.0 and later.

`JSObject` is a class—that is, it defines a type of object. You can think of `JSObject` like the JavaScript objects with which you are familiar: the Window object, the Document object, and so forth. For Java programmers, `JSObject` provides a way to communicate directly with JavaScript. `JSObject` manages translation details, converting text strings, booleans (`true`/`false` values), arrays, and other data types between Java and JavaScript.

`JSObject` also provides methods, such as `eval()` and `call()`, which enable Java to execute JavaScript statements and function calls. Java's `eval()` is similar to JavaScript's `eval()`. It evaluates a JavaScript expression. For example, the Java Remote Control that you viewed earlier uses the following statements to pass a value to the `slider()` function, which is written in JavaScript and is contained in the page that hosts the applet:

```
JSObject jso = JSObject.getWindow(this);
jso.eval("slider(" + jCSlider1.getValue() + ")");
```

As you can see, these statements, written in Java, look very similar to JavaScript. The two languages have many similarities, at least on the surface. These statements run every time the slider's value is changed. The object `jso` is of the type `JSObject`. The `getWindow()` method is used to return a reference to the window in which the applet is running. The second statement assembles a function call to the `slider()` function, based on the value returned from the `jCSlider1` slide control. For example, if the slide control contained a value of `"12"`, then the following JavaScript function call would be made:
`slider(12)`.

On the JavaScript side of things, the Web page contains the following function:

```
function slider(theSetting) {
  document.theForm.txtSetting.value = theSetting;
}
```

The value passed to this function from Java is simply placed into the `txtSetting` text box.

# Topic 6B

## Communicating With Director Shockwave Movies

*Shockwave* is an applet format developed by Macromedia. Shockwave applets can be developed using Macromedia's various authoring tools, including Director, Authorware, and Flash. To play Shockwave applets in a browser, you need to install extensions (such as plug-ins or ActiveX controls) in your Web browser. In some cases, different extensions need to be installed to run different types of Shockwave applets (depending on whether the applet was created in Director, Authorware or Flash). Also, some operating systems and Web browsers automatically install Shockwave on the user's computer so the user needn't be bothered with a separate installation.

Shockwave applets created in Director are called movies—in line with Director's movie-making metaphor. In Director, the applet developer (or author) constructs a movie using a Score and Cast members. Director includes a comprehensive programming language called Lingo, which tends to provide a bit more flexibility than the programming capabilities provided in Authorware, and much more than the very limited programming capabilities provided in Flash.

Lingo can directly perform network operations, such as reading and writing files—although for security reasons, these capabilities are limited when a movie is running as an applet. (In addition to running as applets, movies can also be compiled to run as stand-alone applications.)

However, a movie applet can read parameters passed to it from a Web page, and can send navigation requests to a Web page in the form of a URL. A movie applet could thus be used as a navigation control (to move to another Web page) or could use the JavaScript URL to send JavaScript commands to the JavaScript interpreter.

**Shockwave:**
*An applet format developed by Macromedia. Shockwave applets are played through a Shockwave plug-in or ActiveX control.*

# TASK 6B-1:

## Examining a Shockwave Movie

**Setup:** To perform this task, make sure you have installed the Shockwave for Director extensions for your Web browser. If you do not already have the required plug-in or ActiveX control, you can obtain it at **www.macromedia.com**. (If you attempt to access a page that contains a Shockwave movie, you will be prompted to install Shockwave if it is not present on your system.)

1. From the JavaScript Exploratorium's main menu, **display the page for Communicating With Applets And Applications.**

2. **Click on Shockwave** to display a page that contains an example slider control that is implemented using Shockwave.

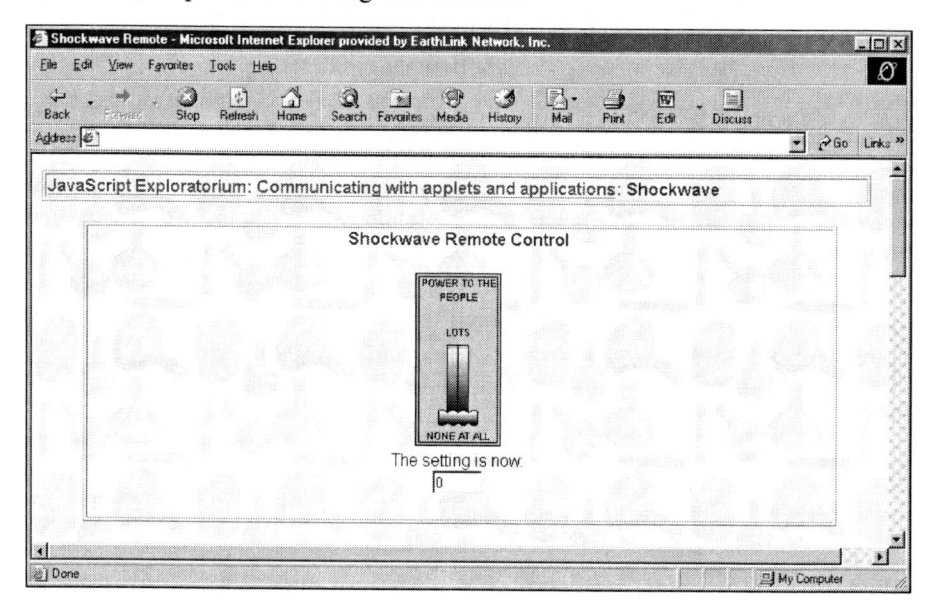

3. **Drag the handle for the controller up.** When you release the mouse button, a new setting appears in the text box below the slider control. If you drag the slider all the way to the top, its value is 255. If you drag the slider all the way to the bottom, its value is 0.

4. **Examine the code listing for the slider control:**

```
<script language="JavaScript"><!--
function slider(theSetting) {
  document.theForm.txtSetting.value = theSetting;
}
// -->
</script>

<div align="center">
  <p><b><font color="#0000ff" face="Arial, Helvetica, sans-serif">
  Shockwave Remote Control</font></b></p>
  <table width="150" border="0">
    <tr align="center">
      <td><object
```

```html
        <td><object
            classid=clsid:166B1BCA-3F9C-11CF-8075-444553540000
codebase=http://download.macromedia.com/pub/shockwave/cabs⇒
          /director/sw.cab#version=7,0,0,0
            height=160
            width=80
            border=1>

          <param name="sw1" value="POWER TO THE PEOPLE">
          <param name="sw2" value="LOTS">
          <param name="sw3" value="NONE AT ALL">
          <param name="sw4" value="0">
          <param name="sw5" value="255">
          <param name="SRC" value="Control.dcr">
          <param name="AutoStart" value="TRUE">
          <param name="Sound" value="TRUE">
          <param name="SaveDisabled" value="FALSE">
          <param name="logo" value="TRUE">
          <param name="progress" value="TRUE">
          <param name="PowerMenuEnabled" value="TRUE">
          <param name="swModifyReport" value="FALSE">

         <embed
             src="Control.dcr"
         align="baseline"
         border="1"
         width="80"
         height="160"
         pluginspage= ⇒
         "http://www.macromedia.com/shockwave/download/"
         sw1="POWER TO THE PEOPLE"
         sw2="LOTS"
         sw3="NONE AT ALL"
         sw4="0"
         sw5="255"
         SRC="Control.dcr"
         AutoStart="TRUE"
         Sound="TRUE" >

    </embed>
        </object></td>
    </tr>
    <tr align="center">
      <td>
        <form action="" name="theForm" >
          <font face="Arial, Helvetica, sans-serif">
                The setting is now:
          <input name="txtSetting" width = 5 value=0 size=5>
          </font>
        </form>
      </td>
    </tr>
  </table>
</div>
```

Essentially, the code that enables the applet to communicate with the Web page is in two sections:

- The first section is the Object and Embed tags—a combination of both is used to support Internet Explorer and Netscape Navigator—and the Param tags, which specify values to be passed to the applet.
- The second section is the slider function, which enables communication with the applet. When the user changes the position of the control, the applet calls this JavaScript function, passing it the new value of the slider control. The function responds by copying the value to the txtSetting text box, although it could conceivably perform any number of other tasks based on the value, even passing the value to another applet if need called for it.

## Sending External Parameters Through Embed and Object

Before the movie actually begins running, you can specify that certain parameters be passed to it. You do this by using the <PARAM> tag. For example, you can specify that the movie should automatically start running when it finishes loading by specifying the following parameter:

```
<PARAM NAME="AutoStart" VALUE="TRUE">
```

AutoStart is one of many predefined parameters present for every movie. If you do not specify a value for these parameters, a default value is used. Shockwave also provides several generic parameters that you can use for your own purposes. These parameters are "sw1" through "sw9." For example, suppose you had created a movie that implemented a two-player game, such as checkers or chess. You might want to display the players' names on the chess board. You could use sw1 and sw2 to pass the players' names from HTML to the Shockwave movie. Of course, the movie would have to be programmed to use the values passed in sw1 and sw2 as the players' names.

Navigator uses the Embed tag to link to the Shockwave plug-in, whereas Internet Explorer uses the Object tag. It is possible to use both tags in combination to support both types of browsers. When you create a Shockwave applet in Director, an option in the Save As Shockwave dialog box enables Director to automatically create the necessary HTML to do this. Later in this topic, you will view a sample Web page that supports both types of browser.

Note that it is also possible to save some Shockwave movies as Java applets. In this situation, the rules for embedding Java applets apply.

Parameters are read in the Shockwave movie using three Lingo functions: externalParamValue, externalParamName, and externalParamCount.

## Providing Interactivity Between a Movie and JavaScript

To provide interactivity between the applet and JavaScript, the applet must be able to communicate to JavaScript when the value of the slider has been changed by the user.

## Using Lingo to Communicate With the Host Page

One way to communicate with JavaScript is to call a JavaScript function using Director's built-in scripting language, called Lingo. Lingo has several functions that enable a Shockwave applet to communicate with a browser. One of these is Lingo's `GoToNetPage` function, which enables Director movies to use the default browser to go to a specific URL. You can use the `javascript:` protocol identifier to specify one or more JavaScript statements. The example in the JavaScript Exploratorium uses a function call (to the slider function) to pass a parameter that contains the value of the slider control.

Another way to communicate from Lingo to the host page is to use the `ExternalEvent` function. `ExternalEvent` enables you to pass a function name to JavaScript. In Internet Explorer, the function name is received as an event. Therefore, you must provide an event handler to accept the event. Navigator simply calls the specified function.

Because the `GoToNetPage` function behaves the same way in both browsers, it is simpler to call JavaScript functions using `GoToNetPage` with a `javascript:` URL than it is to use `ExternalEvent`.

## Using JavaScript to Communicate With the Movie Object

The `GoToNetPage` function enables you to communicate from the movie object to JavaScript, but suppose you wanted to communicate in the other direction—from JavaScript to the movie?

The Movie object provides a number of methods that enable JavaScript to control the movie, including the following:

- `Play()` starts the movie if it is stopped.
- `Stop()` stops the movie if it is playing.
- `Rewind()` rewinds the movie to its beginning.
- `GetCurrentFrame()` returns an integer identifying the number of the current frame in the movie.
- `EvalScript(scriptString)` enables you to pass a Lingo script from JavaScript to the movie. The script runs immediately in the movie. This method can return a result back to JavaScript, if the `EvalScript` handler in the movie has been programmed to do so.

## NetLingo

Lingo includes many other functions that enable Shockwave movies to perform a variety of networking tasks. Collectively, these functions are known as NetLingo.

## Topic 6C

### Communicating with ActiveX

Microsoft's ActiveX technology can also be used to embed controls in a Web page. *ActiveX controls* have been used for several years in Microsoft Windows applications as a way to share common functionality among applications.

**ActiveX control:**
*A type of software module that uses Microsoft's Component Object Model (COM) software technology. Like Java applets, an ActiveX control can be automatically downloaded and executed by Web browsers that support their use.*

ActiveX controls must be registered on the computer on which they run. Essentially, they become an extension of the system itself. When a Web page calls for a particular ActiveX control, the system can look in its Registry to determine if the control is already installed (obviating the need to download and install it).

ActiveX controls are embedded using the `<OBJECT>` tag. Most of the more sophisticated HTML editors provide a facility for embedding ActiveX controls in a Web page during authoring. When you add an ActiveX control, the editor presents a list of available ActiveX controls that are registered on that system. When you select the control that you want to embed, the editor automatically constructs the necessary HTML to uniquely identify the control. An example is shown below:

```
<OBJECT name     = Remote
        classid  = "clsid:2F214465-E605-11D2-9883-00105A04BB51"
        codebase = xRemote.cab
        width    = 143
        height   = 90
        align    = center
        hspace   = 0
        vspace   = 0>
</OBJECT>
```

The value of the `classid` property is a unique identification number that Windows assigns to every ActiveX control. This number is also sometimes called a GUID (Global Unique Identifier—more often pronounced goo-id than gwid). Typically, the HTML editor automatically enters this number for you, which, as you can imagine, is a good thing.

The `codebase` property identifies where the Web browser will find the ActiveX control. If the control is not already installed in the user's system, then it is downloaded from the URL specified in this property.

The `width` and `height` of the control are specified in pixels. These properties specify the size of the rectangle in which the control will appear on the Web page. The `align` property specifies how the control will be aligned within its rectangle. The `hspace` and `vspace` properties identify how much padding or border space will surround the control.

Because ActiveX controls are not directly supported by Netscape browsers, other types of applets (such as Java applets) are sometimes preferred over ActiveX controls. For situations that require direct access to the operating system, and for those in which Internet Explorer is the only browser that must be supported, ActiveX controls provide a good means of extending the capabilities of Web pages.

# TASK 6C-1:

## Examining an ActiveX Control

**Setup:** To perform this task, you must use an ActiveX-enabled Web browser, such as Internet Explorer.

1. From the JavaScript Exploratorium's main menu, **display the page for Communicating With Applets And Applications.**

2. **Click on ActiveX** to display a page that contains an example of a slider control that is implemented using ActiveX

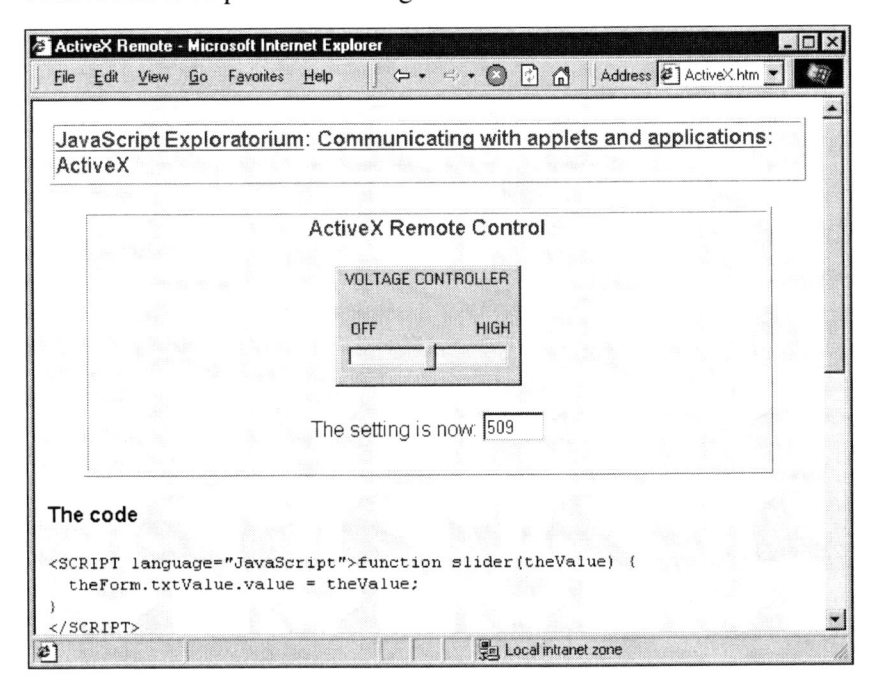

3. **Drag the slider control to different positions** to observe how the value in the text box is updated.

4. **Examine the code listing at the bottom of the Web page.**

    ```
    <SCRIPT language="JavaScript">function slider(theValue) {
      theForm.txtValue.value = theValue;
    }
    </SCRIPT>
    <OBJECT name     = Remote
            classid  = ⇒
    "clsid:2F214465-E605-11D2-9883-00105A04BB51"
            codebase = xRemote.cab
            width    = 143
            height   = 90
            align    = center
            hspace   = 0
            vspace   = 0>
    </OBJECT>

    <SCRIPT language="JavaScript">
      Remote.Title="VOLTAGE CONTROLLER";
    ```

*Lesson 6: Communicating With Applets* **125**

```
Remote.MinTitle="OFF";
Remote.MaxTitle="HIGH";
Remote.MinVal="0";
Remote.MaxVal="1000";

</SCRIPT>

<FORM action="" name=theForm>

  <FONT face="Arial, Helvetica, sans-serif">
    The setting is now:
  </FONT>

  <INPUT type=text name=txtValue size=5>

</FORM>
```

Like the other applets you examined in this lesson, the ActiveX control calls a JavaScript slider( ) function when the slider is moved, passing to the function the new setting of the control.

An Object tag embeds the control in the Web page, assigning the control the name "Remote." JavaScript can refer to the object using this name. In this example, a script sets properties of the control (Title, MinTitle, MaxTitle, and so forth) by referring directly to the Remote object.

## Summary

In this lesson, you used a sample Java applet, Shockwave movie, and ActiveX control, and you examined how JavaScript communicated with them.

## Lesson Review

**6A** Briefly describe the elements necessary to include a Java applet in a Web page and enable two-way communication between the applet and JavaScript.

**6B** Briefly describe the elements necessary to include a Shockwave movie in a Web page and enable two-way communication between the movie and JavaScript.

**6C** Briefly describe the elements necessary to include an ActiveX control in a Web page and enable two-way communication between the control and JavaScript.

YOUR NOTES:

# JavaScript and Server Applications

## APPENDIX A

## Communicating With Server Applications

In general, there are two types of applications that enable a Web server to interact with clients and perform processing on behalf of clients: applications and server-side scripts that use Common Gateway Interface (CGI) to communicate with Web clients; and processes that run as an extension to the server software. Server extensions are implemented through a standard interface such as Netscape's Server API (NSAPI) or Microsoft's Information Server API (ISAPI). (An API is an application programmer's interface, which enables different programs or program modules to communicate with each other.)

## CGI

*CGI* is a fairly simple standard that enables many different types of scripting or programming tools to be used to develop server applications. Server applications can be simple console-mode applications (no windowed user interface) or they can be windowed applications. The main requirement is that such applications adhere to the input/output standard set by UNIX applications.

CGI applications read requests from command-line parameters passed to the program when it runs. A Web client submits a request to server applications by specifying the name of the program that should run on the server, along with parameters that define the nature of the request. It is not unusual to see such communication going on if you keep an eye on the location bar in your browser (the long text box that typically appears near the top of the browser window). For example, a search at **www.yahoo.com** for the text "CGI" produced the following URL:

`http://search.yahoo.com/bin/search?p=CGI`

This simple request identifies the search application (search.yahoo.com/bin/search) and the search parameter (p=CGI). The question mark separates the parameter list from the name of the search application. Apparently Yahoo! has a server script or application named search, and the p=CGI parameter specifies the text to be searched for.

Entering "CGI script" into Yahoo!'s search engine produced the following text in the location bar:

`http://search.yahoo.com/bin/search?p=CGI+script`

**Common Gateway Interface (CGI):**
*A standard that describes how scripting languages and other programming tools can communicate with server applications.*

As you can see, spaces are replaced with plus signs to make the text string compatible with CGI.

Server applications can perform a wide variety of tasks. Often server applications serve as data brokers, providing Web clients with access to a database application. In this scenario, the database might actually be stored on the Web server, or it might be on a separate, remote database server. In the latter situation, the server application serves as a go-between, processing requests from the Web client, passing them on to a remote database server, and formatting information returned from the remote database server into an HTML format that can be displayed by a Web client. Because such Web applications are processed in three separate locations or tiers, they are called three-tiered applications. An example of the data flow in a three-tiered application is shown in the figure below:

***multi-tiered application:*** *Multiple applications, running on various computers that are connected through a network (such as the Internet), working together to perform various aspects of database management.*

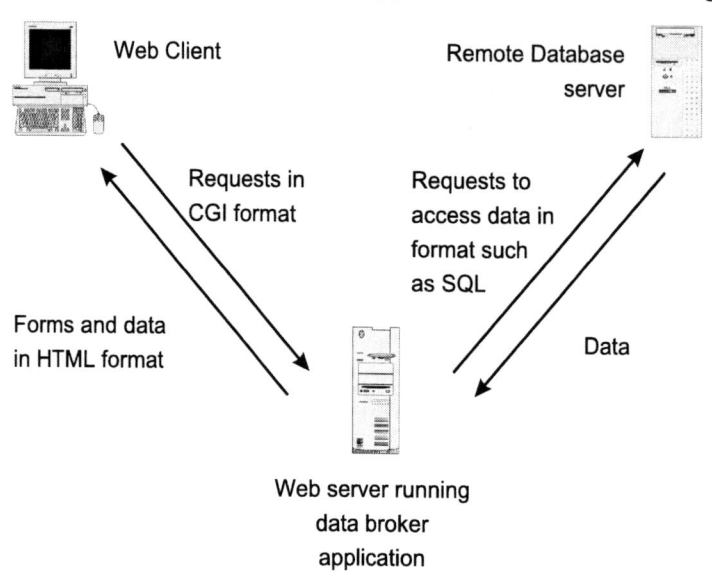

**Figure A-1:** *A three-tiered application, showing its data flow.*

## Identifying Examples of Possible Server Applications and Submitting a Request to a Server Application

Take a minute to review the following:

1. In the space provided, identify examples of possible server applications. (It might help to think of Web sites that you've visited, such as Amazon or Yahoo!.) Also add examples of server applications that other students identify.

   _____
   _____
   _____
   _____

2. From the JavaScript Exploratorium's main menu, click on Communicating With Applets And Applications.

3. Click on Server Applications. This page displays a simple form that enables you to send information to a server application.

4. Enter your name in the text box, and click on Submit. The server application returns the following results. Observe that the Address bar contains the CGI request that was sent to the server application.

```
CGI DEMO

This report was generated by the CGIDEMO server application, as requested by Brian

Information from the server

Environment variables:

Query string...... txtName=Brian&Submit=Submit
Name of server.... wilson
Server protocol... HTTP/1.1
Port.............. 80
Server software... Microsoft-IIS/4.0
Server OS......... -- not available --
Version of CGI.... CGI/1.1
Request method.... GET
Path translated... C:\WINDOWS\Desktop\Work\Adv JavaScript Course\Course Data
Referring URL..... http://wilson/Explore/Applets/CGI.htm
Name of script.... /cgi-bin/cgidemo.exe
Authentication.... -- not available --
Path information.. -- not available --
Mime types........ application/vnd.ms-excel, application/vnd.ms-powerpoint, */*
Remote host....... 155.40.104.49
```

5. Examine the code listing below. This is the HTML that displayed the request form from the previous page. The form tag's action field specifies the name of the server application that should run when the form is submitted. The browser automatically appended data from the form to the URL to create the URL shown in the graphic above.

```
<FORM name=theForm action="/scripts/cgidemo.exe">
  Enter your name in the text box below and click on Submit.
  <INPUT name=txtName size=30><BR>
  <INPUT name=Submit type=submit value="Submit">
</FORM>
```

6. Exit the browser application.

YOUR NOTES:

# SOLUTIONS

# LESSON 1

## Task 1A-1 Page 7

**1. Does it contain an error?**

Yes. Instead of comparing the value of 75 stored in num to the numeric value 100, the if statement assigns 100 into the variable because of the single equals sign (=). Thus, the comparison is never made, and the if statement always returns true.

**2. Does it contain an error?**

Yes. The today Date object attempts to use getFullYear as a property, not a method.

**3. Does it contain an error?**

Yes. Although the use of single- and double-quotation marks to denote string data is OK, the variable Response isn't concatenated to the end of the string—the plus sign is missing.

**4. Does it contain an error?**

No, but it isn't formatted in such a way as to easily see that the nesting of the if statements is correctly coded.

**5. Does it contain an error?**

Yes. The parentheses aren't nested correctly—the closing parenthesis after the variable COLA should be removed (or an initial opening parenthesis added).

## Task 1B-1 Page 9

**8. Did the debugger find any other errors?**

No. This time, the document loaded successfully. The debugger did not appear.

## Task 1B-3 Page 16

**9. Did the highlighted area move? Where?**

Yes, the area moved to divBy(4), the next function call.

**What code (if any) was processed? How can you tell?**

All the code in the multBy() function was processed. Checking the value of output in the Command window shows that multBy() added characters to the output string.

Solutions 133

## Task 1B-4 Page 18

7. **True or False? The line of code marking the breakpoint is executed before processing is stopped by the debugger.**

   *False. Processing stops just before the line of code marking the breakpoint. Otherwise, the* `<BR>` *tag would appear at the end of the string displayed in the Command window for the variable* `output`.

## Task 1B-5 Page 21

3. **What changes did you notice?**

   *Whenever processing took place within the function definitions, a message appeared in the Call Stack window stating that the current context was at the level of the function. Once processing returned to the global level, however, the listing for the function in the Call Stack window disappeared.*

5. **Can you think of situations where it would be important to view the function call stack while debugging code?**

   *For functions that use temporary variables created by other "parent" functions, it would be good to know that the parent function was active when the data was needed.*

## Task 1B-6 Page 23

6. **Can you think of situations in which viewing a list of running documents would be useful?**

   *Answers might include: in situations where you needed to observe how JavaScript opens and closes Window objects, when complicated frameset documents are used, or when included JavaScript files are needed.*

## Apply Your Knowledge 1-1 Page 30

1. **A solution to this exercise is provided in the answer section.**

```
catch(excpt)
  {
  if(typeof(excpt) == "string")
    {
    alert(excpt.substr(1));
    frm.elements[excpt.charAt(0)].focus();
    }
  else if(excpt.description)
    {
    alert("Error for IE user: " + excpt.description);
    }
  else
    {
    alert("Error for NN user: " + excpt.message);
    }
  }
```

# LESSON REVIEW 1

## Topic 1-A

**Name some common coding errors made by JavaScript developers.**

*Answers might include: inconsistent letter casing; using undefined variables; using an incorrect number of brackets or parentheses; using a single equals sign in a comparative expression; omitting concatenation operators; and using a property as a method or a method as a property.*

## Topic 1-B

**List the main features of Internet Explorer's script debugger.**
- *The Break At Next Statement menu choice.*
- *The* `debugger` *keyword.*
- *The Step Through buttons.*
- *Breakpoints.*
- *The Command window.*
- *The Call Stack window.*
- *The Running Documents window.*

**Which did you find most useful?**

*Answers will vary.*

## Topic 1-C

**Is handling errors with the try...catch construct an either/or proposition (in that you can work only with unexpected errors or define errors with the `throw` clause, but not both)? Why or why not?**

*By checking the status of an execption variable with the `typeof()` method, you can branch code such that both unexpected errors and thrown errors can be handled from within a single try...catch construct.*

# Lesson Review 2

## Topic 2-A

Write a statement that uses the `Object()` constructor function to create an object named `myNewObject`.

*myNewObject = new Object();*

## Topic 2-B

Write an object constructor function called `Rock` that accepts no arguments and creates an object with three properties—type, origin, and weight—each of which is initialized to contain the string value "not known." Also write a statement to create an instance of the Rock object called "aNewRock."

```
function Rock() {
   this.type = "not known";
   this.origin = "not known";
   this.weight = "not known";
}

aNewRock = new Rock( );
```

## Topic 2-C

Write a statement that you would use to declare a method called `calcDensity()` within an object constructor function. The `calcDensity` method refers to a function named `Rock_calcDensity()`.

*this.calcDensity = Rock_calcDensity;*

# Lesson 3

## Task 3A-1 Page 52

1. In the space provided below, identify possible uses for arrays. Use the examples:

   *Answers may include:*

   *Arrays could hold lookup tables such as zip codes, shipping rates, and so forth.*

   *Arrays could hold information about parts in a parts inventory—such as storage bin location, quantity of parts in stock, and so forth.*

136  JavaScript: Advanced Programming (Second Edition)

# Lesson Review 3

## Topic 3-A

**Explain why it is beneficial to place data within array structures.**

*Arrays provide data structures that lend themselves to automated processing.*

## Topic 3-B

**Write one or more statements that create an array named `myJobs`, and populate it with the following entries:**
- Butcher
- Baker
- Web Developer

*Answers may vary, but will either use a custom object constructor function, the Array() constructor, or will assign an array literal to a variable. Examples are shown below:*

CUSTOM OBJECT CONSTRUCTOR:

```
function customArray(theLength) {
   this.length = theLength;
   for (i=1; i<=theLength; i++) this[i] = null;
   return this;
}
var myJobs = new customArray(3);
myJobs[1] = "Butcher";
myJobs[2] = "Baker";
myJobs[3] = "Web Developer";
```

ARRAY CONSTRUCTOR:

```
myJobs = new Array("Butcher","Baker","Web Developer");
```

ARRAY LITERAL:

```
var myJobs = ["Butcher","Baker","Web Developer"];
```

## Topic 3-C

**Write a statement that deletes the data value held in the third element in the array `myFavoriteThings` without deleting the element itself.**

`delete myFavoriteThings[2];`

**Write a statement that deletes all elements (so that its length is zero) from the array `myFavoriteThings`, without destroying the array.**

`myFavoriteThings.length = 0;`

## Topic 3-D

**Given the following statements, what statement would you write to put the value "50" into the third column, first row of the matrix?**

```
tictactoe = new Array(3);
tictactoe[0] = new Array(3);
tictactoe[1] = new Array(3);
tictactoe[2] = new Array(3);
```

*tictactoe[2][0] (or possibly tictactoe[0][2] if you consider the row coordinate to be the first coordinate).*

# Lesson 4

## Task 4A-1 Page 71

**3. Were you successful?**

*No. Neither file contains the data.*

**4. How is the data from zodiac.js included in the DTProject.html application?**

*It is linked into DTLeft.html via a <SCRIPT> tag whose SRC attribute is set to zodiac.js.*

**Is the data in zodiac.js hard-coded into the array, or is it processed from a delimited file? Why?**

*The data is processed from a delimited file, with function calls sending each line of data for processing. If the data were hard-coded, each data point would be explicitly defined in a JavaScript assignment statement placing the data into an array element.*

## Task 4A-2 Page 74

**2. How many records are in the data table?**

*45.*

**How many fields are in each record?**

*5.*

**What is the purpose of the first record?**

*Instead of holding data similar to the other records, it holds the names of the data fields. Therefore, it is a header record.*

**4. What does this code block do?**

*It creates 45 elements for the three arrays, and instantiates an Array object into each element, forming the arrays' second dimension.*

# Lesson Review 4

## Topic 4-A

**What are the three main activities on which data table manipulation is based?**

*Selecting, sorting, and searching.*

## Topic 4-B

**What is the impact of using identical index numbers for the fields listed in the Select object of a data table selecting function, and the field ordering of the data table housed in a two-dimensional array used to manipulate the table?**

*Because the index numbering for the field list in the Select object and the data table are identical, the Option object's* `selected` *property can be used in an* `if` *statement to allow assembly of selected data items into the table row being formed for output.*

## Topic 4-C

**How is a pointer array used in crafting a single-term search function?**

*After assembling a series of record numbers in the pointer array by cycling through the data table array and testing the specified field value for each record, the pointer array's values are used in the output generating code to list the criterion-meeting records in the HTML table.*

## Topic 4-D

**How can you use a temporary sort array to sort a data table?**

*The temporary sort array is used to collect the data values for sorting. Appended to the end of each data value is the record number from which it came. Once sorted, the record numbers are detached from their data values, and then collected into the pointer array. The pointer array is then used to order the rows in the body of an HTML table.*

# Lesson Review 5

## Topic 5-A

**Briefly explain why cookies are beneficial, and explain their limitations.**

*Cookies enable values to be stored on a Web client's local storage, for retrieval at any later time. This is useful because variables and objects are deleted from memory when the user moves to another page or exits the browser application. This enables JavaScript developers to maintain persistent settings or values that are associated with a particular Web page or site, such as a user's name, preferences, or choices.*

*Cookies are associated with a particular computer and browser version, which might be a disadvantage for users who use multiple Web clients or computers. The size and number of cookies are limited. A cookie might be purged automatically if its space is needed by another cookie.*

## Topic 5-B

**Write an example statement that stores a value within a cookie.**

*Answers may vary, but they must include an assignment to* `document.cookie` *of a string that includes a* `"name="` *phrase and a* `"value="` *phrase. Optionally, the cookie string can also include phrases that specify an expiration date (in GMT string format), path, domain, and secure attribute. All phrases must be separated by a semicolon. A simple example is:*

```
document.cookie = "name=bowlingAvg; value=253";
```

## Topic 5-C

**Briefly describe the approach for reading cookies.**

1. Read `document.cookie` *to get a string containing all of the page's cookies, which are separated by semicolons.*
2. *Divide the string into substrings at the semicolons.*
3. *Read each of these substrings up to the first equals sign to determine the name of the cookie.*
4. *Once you've found the cookie you're looking for, extract the part of the substring that follows the equals sign. This is the cookie's value.*
5. *If you've stored multiple items in a single cookie, divide the cookie value up into substrings at the characters that you used to separate them.*
6. *Use* `unescape()` *to decode escape characters.*

## Topic 5-D

**Briefly describe the approach for deleting cookies.**

*Set the cookie's contents to an empty string and give the cookie an expiration date of some time in the past.*

# Lesson Review 6

## Topic 6-A

**Briefly describe the elements necessary to include a Java applet in a Web page and enable two-way communication between the applet and JavaScript.**

*Use the Applet tag to embed the applet in the Web page. The* `mayscript` *field must be included with the tag to specify that JavaScript can communicate with the applet.*

*Use the Param tag to specify custom applet settings.*

*Provide one or more JavaScript functions that the applet can call to respond to events.*

## Topic 6-B

**Briefly describe the elements necessary to include a Shockwave movie in a Web page and enable two-way communication between the movie and JavaScript.**

*Use the Object and Embed tags to embed the movie in the Web page.*

*Use the Param tag to specify custom movie settings.*

*Provide one or more JavaScript functions that the applet can call to respond to events.*

## Topic 6-C

**Briefly describe the elements necessary to include an ActiveX control in a Web page and enable two-way communication between the control and JavaScript.**

*Use the Object tag to embed the control in the Web page, assigning the applet a name using the Name field.*

*Use JavaScript to directly set public properties of the ActiveX control.*

*Provide one or more JavaScript functions that the control can call in response to events.*

YOUR NOTES:

# GLOSSARY

**ActiveX control**
A type of software module that uses Microsoft's Component Object Model (COM) software technology. Like Java applets, an ActiveX control can be automatically downloaded and executed by Web browsers that support their use.

**applet**
A small program that is embedded within a Web page. Applets run on client computers, rather than on a Web server.

**array**
A list or collection of variables, called elements, that are identified by a shared name, with specific elements in the array identified by an index value.

**array literals**
A syntactic method of populating arrays as you create them.

**breakpoints**
Places in your code where you can stop the execution of code to check variable values.

**Command window**
A pop-up window, opened from the Debugging toolbar, that enables you to determine the values held in variables as you step through your code.

**Common Gateway Interface (CGI)**
A standard that describes how scripting languages and other programming tools can communicate with server applications.

**cookie**
A small chunk of string data that is stored in a Web client's local disk storage. Cookies are typically used to hold user preferences or special data that needs to be maintained across multiple Web pages.

**delimited file**
A data table whose records are presented in rows having fields separated by a symbol, such as a comma.

**event**
An action that causes a function to run. Events are typically instigated by users. For example, an onClick event occurs when a user points at a particular object (by using a mouse) and clicks a mouse button.

**header record**
Usually the first record of a data table housed in a two-dimensional array table, used to store the name of the array's fields.

**matrix**
An array limited to a single row that contains any number of columns.

**method**
A function that "belongs" to an object.

**methods**
Functions stored as properties of an object.

**multi-tiered application**
Multiple applications, running on various computers that are connected through a network (such as the Internet), working together to perform various aspects of database management.

**Object() constructor**
A special method (a function belonging to an object) that is used to initialize an object when it is created. Tasks performed by the object constructor include such things as creating properties, assigning initial values to properties, identifying the object's methods, and so forth.

**parallel arrays**
Sets of arrays that are the same length, with related data stored at the same index in each array.

**pointer array**
An array used to house record numbers so that the rows of a data table can be reordered.

# GLOSSARY

**property**

An attribute of an object, such as width, name, and so forth. You can set a property (that is, a value can be assigned to it) and you can get a property (when you read its value).

**Shockwave**

An applet format developed by Macromedia. Shockwave applets are played through a Shockwave plug-in or ActiveX control.

**sort array**

A one-dimensional array that has as its elements the data values of the field being sorted, along with a means of determining the position of the data item in the data table from which it was extracted.

# INDEX

## A
ActiveX, 124-126
applets
 communicating with Java, 116-117
 interactivity, 118-119
 setting parameters, 117-118
 Shockwave, 119-122
Array() constructor, 54-55
arrays, 50
 changing size, 51
 creating, 51, 52
 deleting elements, 57-58
 destroying, 58-59
 indices, 50
 literals, 56
 multi-dimensional, 51, 59
 nested, 60-62
 nesting within an object, 62-66
 parallel, 59-60
 populating, 51, 52
 population at creation, 56
 simulating with objects, 53-54
 string indices, 55-56
 uses, 50-51
 working with, 51-52

## C
Command window, 15-16
Common Gateway Interface (CGI), 129
constructor function
 method creation, 40-46
cookies, 94-97
 assigning a domain, 99
 assigning a path, 99
 assigning an expiration date, 98-99
 deleting, 107-112
 limitations, 97
 practical uses, 97
 processing, 102
 reading, 102, 104-105
 storing, 98
 storing multiple items, 105-107
 storing values in, 100-102
custom objects
 creating, 35
 data types contained in, 35-37
 defined, 34
 events, 35
 methods, 34
 properties, 34

## D
data manipulation
 searching, 81-85
 selecting, 77-80
 sorting, 86-90
data tables, 70-72
 as Array objects, 72
 delimited files and, 75-77
 hard-coding of, 72-75
domain field, 99

## E
escape(), 98
events, 34
Exception object, 24-27

## F
functions
 constructor, 37-39

## H
header record, 72-75

## I
indexOf(), 103-104

## L
length(), 103-104
Lingo, 123

## M
methods, 34, 40-46
Microsoft Windows Script Debugger
 activating, 11-14
 breakpoints, 18-20
 Call Stack window, 21-22
 defined, 8-11
 enabling, 8-11
 Running Documents window, 22-24
 Step Through tools, 15-17
movies
 external parameters, 122

## N
NetLingo, 123

## O
object constructor, 35
objects, 34
 cookie, 94-97

## P
path field, 100
pointer array, 87-88
pointer arrays, 73
properties, 34

## R
RegExp object, 81

## S
scripting errors
 assignment/comparison, 5
 concatenation symbol, 5
 letter casing, 3
 list of, 2-8
 properties/methods, 5-6
 unbalanced brackets, 3-4
 unbalanced parentheses, 4
 undefined variables, 2-3
secure field, 100
Shockwave, 119-122
split(), 103
Step Into, 15-17
Step Out, 15-17

*Index* 145

# INDEX

Step Over, 15-17
substring(), 103-104

## T

throw, 27-30
try...catch, 24-27
  throwing exceptions, 27-30